TEMPTATIONS MEN FACE

Temptations Men Face

TOM EISENMAN

KINGSWAY PUBLICATIONS
EASTBOURNE

British Library Cataloguing in Publication Data

Eisenman, Tom
    Temptations men face
    1. Christian life. Temptation
    I. Title
    248.4

    ISBN 0–86065–895–3

Printed in Great Britain for
KINGSWAY PUBLICATIONS LTD
1 St Anne's Road, Eastbourne, E Sussex BN21 3UN by
Courier International Ltd, Tiptree, Essex
Reproduced from the original text by arrangement with
InterVarsity Press

To three holy men,
my friends, Earl Grice, Bob Oerter
and Joe Bayly, who have tempted me
with righteousness, and to my parents,
Bob and Marilynn, with love.

Acknowledgments

A number of friends have given me help in forming and editing material in this book. Jim, Dave, Bruce, Dick and Tom supported me in prayer in our Thursday morning men's Bible study and have been a constant source of creative insight as we have discussed together many of the topics included here. I have received manuscript help from Dr. Jay Lindsay, Dr. James Osterhaus, Gwen Brown, Peggy Parker and my wife, Judie. Andrew Le Peau at InterVarsity Press has been an honest friend whose clear thinking and loving encouragement have kept me writing during the difficult times.

Preface

Historians writing about religion in our day will characterize the late 1980s as a time when public trust in Christian leaders plummeted to an all-time low.

My young son Josh watched a recent news report which exposed Jimmy Swaggart as a voyeur, turned to me and said, "Dad, you just can't trust anybody anymore." It's not that Josh is a devoted follower of Swaggart's ministry. But he knows who the man is and what he is supposed to stand for. It is a sad commentary on the state of the church when children feel they have to give up trust in Christian leaders at the age of thirteen.

A friend of mine who pastors a church in Colorado Springs found out that his young sons were telling kids at school that he was a counselor instead of a pastor. He questioned his boys about it. They told their dad they were afraid the other kids would think the wrong things about him if they said he was a pastor. They wanted the other kids to know that he was really a good dad.

Certainly the problem of moral indiscretion is not a new one for the church. If there had been investigative television reporters in David's time, his transgression with Bathsheba would have made world news. David might have had his own show. Human nature is a constant we can usually count on.

So why do men fail? In prominent leaders there appears to be something about the way pride joins success that makes holy living difficult over the long haul. We start believing our press clippings. Joseph R. McAuliffe put it this way: "The strange brew that forms from mixing men with power has to do with the character of the man. Most are snared by the accouterments of success because their value system is not developed sufficiently to handle the weight of glory."[1]

Most of us do not have to deal with the pressures and temptations that result from national prominence. But all of us know what it is like to have the sheer weight of everyday life overwhelm us. Life gets out ahead of the development of our character. When it does, we may be headed for a fall. This is why it is a pressing issue for us to learn to let God build into us strength and heavenly wisdom as we grow toward maturity in Christ. Our developing character has to keep pace with the powerful influences that contend for control over our lives.

The church desperately needs men today whose testimony will echo Paul's before his death, "I have fought the good fight, I have finished the race, I have kept the faith" (2 Tim 4:7). It is not easy to fight the good fight. But our faithful God can build tenacious character into our lives if we are willing to be built. We can be men of integrity, men who can be trusted, men of courage who are willing to fight this tough fight against the temptations that threaten to erode our character and cripple the church.

Our choices have both personal and corporate consequences. We are to be personally faithful, to keep ourselves from being tainted by the world and overpowered by its subtle enticements. This is the way we enter into authentic joy and freedom. This is the way we gain strength and health for effective living. Our faithfulness is also essential to the health and effectiveness of the church. We are to be salt and light. This is the role of the church in our fallen and dying world. We have to be jealous of our reputation. Men who live out their Christian character in the marketplace can help regain the place of proper influence that rightly belongs to the church.

Some might wonder why I chose to write a book on temptation that speaks primarily to men. Certainly it is not that I think men are tempted more than women, or that men are in greater need of help, or that men carry more responsibility than women to live appropriately under God. The reason I am writing this book for men is simple and personal. I am a man. I experience life as a man. The things I've learned have come from my struggles with temptation from a man's point of view. A book like this has to be written from authentic experience. If the book were aimed at a general audience, it would lack authenticity at any point where I attempted to speak in specifics about temptations women face. The book would also have to be by design less practical than I wanted it to be.

It should also be said from the beginning that I do not believe the temptations mentioned in this book are temptations that only men experience or have an interest in reading about. Topics included in the book have been chosen because they are common areas of struggle for men, but a woman's book would very likely include many of the same topics. A woman who read this book would surely gain some help and insight from the temptation topics addressed. A woman might want to read this book to better understand men and why a man may respond the way he does to the power of a particular temptation. I have included a chapter just for women near the end of the book.

Finally, I have written this book largely out of my experience of working with men, counseling men and living as a Christian man in tension with the world. I did not want to write a research treatise. I chose to approach the topic in a personal and practical way. At the same time I promise you that I have worked with a strong sense of responsibility. I believe the things I say are based in Scripture, true of human nature and consistent with common sense. Still, your experience may differ from mine at some points. That's fine. Read the book for the help it will bring. ·

The bench press tests me at the gym. I am always fighting against the heavy bar, trying to press a few more pounds. One thing that has amazed me is that I can press a great deal more weight if I have a friend spotting for me, someone to place his fingers under the bar when the going gets rough. The person spotting me usually does not have to help lift at all. Just knowing he is there makes the difference. Having someone behind me gives me the confidence to work harder and to press on farther than I could go alone.

My hope is that this book will spot you on occasion as you work through it, that just when you thought you could go no farther, some idea or Scripture or experience shared will be the encouragement you need to start fresh and move on to higher ground. You are already courageous. No one who lacks spirit would buy and read a book like this. It takes guts to want to deal with the realities of the Christian life at this deeper level.

The words of the apostle Paul, our brother in Christ and fellow struggler, can be an encouragement to each of us: "Not that I have already obtained all this, or have already been made perfect, but I press on to take hold of that for which Christ Jesus took hold of me. Brothers, I do not consider myself yet to have taken hold of it. But one thing I do: Forgetting what is behind and straining toward what is ahead, I press on toward the goal to win the prize for which God has called me heavenward in Christ Jesus" (Phil 3:12-13).

Let's press on together toward freedom in Christ.

1/SET FREE

*O*nce when I was a young boy I came very close to drowning.
I remember it as vividly today as if it had happened only
yesterday. The mossy smell of the backwater still burns in my
throat and nostrils. My imagination can recreate the horror of
gasping for air and then choking as my mouth and lungs filled
instead with cold, muddy river water.

As a child, I was a weak swimmer. My friends were better
swimmers who coaxed me out with them into a swift backwater
slough of the Mississippi River. I was careful to stay where I
could touch the bottom. But the current was very strong. The
water moved me downstream.

Soon I became frightened and decided to head toward shore.
It was then that the river played a dirty trick on me. As I edged

toward the bank, expecting to walk safely up into shallow water, the channel became deeper instead. I was about thirty feet out. I tried again and again to make it to shore. Panic took over. Finally I rushed toward shore in a foolish, last-ditch effort. In a matter of seconds the water was up to my chin. The current swept me farther down. My toes tried desperately to find a grip in the shifting slime that made up the bottom of that mucky stretch of backwater. I was bobbing, gasping, choking—drowning. And then my arms were flailing wildly as I screamed desperately for help.

Fortunately for me, an older boy on the bank heard my cries. He swam to where I was, took my hand, talked to me to calm me down, and led me more toward the center of the stream and higher ground. Then he helped me back upstream to the place where I had first entered the water. At that point I could walk on my own. I stumbled up on shore and fell in the dirt exhausted, chilled and shivering.

I remember most how utterly confused I had been out there. I recall how drained I felt from fighting with everything I had and making no progress against the powerful stream. And then there was the frightening moment when the thought entered my mind that it might be easier to give up than to go on struggling against the rushing current and the deep, black water.

Emotions like these have come to me many times since that frightening childhood experience. Often they are associated with my struggle against sin. Too many times I have in my weakness been swept downstream in one of the currents of our culture. Certainly I have been out over my head more than I would like. Then I have felt again the fear of drowning in something I could not control.

Every believer from biblical times to the present has fought this fight. These have been men like you and me. They too had the pressures of trying to make a living, raise a family and live out the call of God in their day. They wanted what we want, to grow in grace to maturity in Christ, attaining the knowledge, wisdom and power of God to be faithful and obedient and to know his glorious joy in the moment-by-moment reality of living.

But I think the struggle against sin and its power might be a tougher fight for us now than at almost any other time in recent history. From every direction today we are bombarded with powerful temptations that can lead us away from God. Men used to have to go out of their way to give themselves to sin. Today the possibilities for sin are present absolutely everywhere—in the shopping malls, on TV, in school, at work, in the theaters, in the newspapers and on every page of our magazines. We are exposed daily to an incredible variety of opportunities for disobedience in thought and action. The pervasive stimulation captures our attention and feeds our fantasies. It seems like there is no escape. *consciences seared*

What makes it even harder for us today is that we receive almost no help at all from society. There was a time when behaving sinfully also entailed acting contrary to established cultural norms. But yielding to temptation has become the norm today. Right and wrong drift with the subjective whim of the majority, most of whom have now grown up in an unchurched culture and are a generation beyond those who held Christian values even though they had already given up the faith. The loss of societal support for righteous living means that men and women who choose Christ in our day will have to be part of a counterculture movement. It is always tough to swim upstream against the prevailing current.

Another difficulty is that the temptations we resist today come to us charged with the raw power of advertising and couched in the subtle and perverted genius of worldly persuasion. No age has had to deal with these things as we do. Everything from soft drinks to tires is sold with sex. Powerful and compelling images combine with clever pseudo-rational arguments to convince us that having and experiencing more of the world is what we all need to make us truly happy. The temptations have an intensity about them that drives our conscious and subconscious minds. Modern advertising alone is powerful enough to keep us continually off-balance if we do not learn how to manage its appeals.

Each year when I take a week away to hunt elk in the Colorado wilderness, I am reminded of how intense and constant this pressure of temptation is in my everyday life. The first day or two away I experience a kind of withdrawal. I feel a little nervous, out of my environment, unsure of how I should act now that I have left civilization behind. But by the end of the week I don't want to come back. My heart enjoys the peace of the wilderness. It is so much easier to fellowship with God in an environment free from the common barrage of distractions.

It is good, to a degree, to try to control our environment. We all need peace and rest in our schedules. But escape to the wilderness, as appealing as it may sound, is not the answer. Clearly, Jesus wants us to live in the world, to learn to deal with its seductions and temptations, to find out more about how to build our strength and be effective where we are. He spoke to his father about the disciples saying, "My prayer is not that you take them out of the world but that you protect them from the evil one" (Jn 17:15).

This is really the central issue in this book. How can we live effectively as Christian men in this present world without being overcome by its pressures and enslaved by its powers? How can we live as free men in Christ and bear fruit for the kingdom of God?

Set Free

One of the main characters in C. S. Lewis's *The Voyage of the Dawn Treader* is a terrible kid named Eustace. At one point in the novel Eustace becomes a dragon. Not until he turns into a real, scaly, fire-breathing dragon with ugly dragonish appetites does Eustace realize that all along he has had a dragon personality in human form. Once he sees what he is really like, he wants nothing more than to become a boy again. But how will he be undragoned? It is a problem too big for all the characters in the book except one—Aslan. He is the great lion that Lewis created to be the Christ figure in the Narnia books.

One night Eustace the dragon meets Aslan the lion. Aslan leads him up into the mountains to a beautiful place where there is a garden and a pool. Eustace thinks if he could just get into that clear pool to bathe he might be healed. Then Aslan tells him he must undress before going down into the water. Eustace is confused at first because he is wearing no clothes. But then he thinks he might be able to scratch off a few scales or peel out of his dragonskin like a snake.

In this Eustace is somewhat successful. He gets a few scales off and eventually peels out of a whole layer of skin. Then he heads down toward the pool. At the edge he is shocked when he sees his reflection on the smooth surface. He is still clothed with thick scales and dragonskin. Disappointed but determined, Eustace goes to work on the second skin and eventually peels out of that one too. But to no avail. He finds again that he has another ugly, scaly skin beneath the second layer. He eventually peels several skins off, but each time he finds a similar skin underneath. Finally he is at his wit's end and ready to give up in frustration.

Here the lion tells Eustace *he* will have to undress him. Eustace is afraid of the lion's claws, but he is so desperate by now that he turns over on his back and lets him do it. Aslan pierces Eustace's dragon skin with his sharp claws and peels it all off. It is a terrifying experience for Eustace, but he feels wonderful after being set free from all the heavy, knobby skin and scales.

Aslan carries Eustace down into the water. The pain he had known as a dragon is gone. He realizes, as he splashes in the pool, that he has turned back into a boy. Then Aslan dresses him in new clothes and Eustace returns to make his apologies for how bad he has been. Lewis writes: "It would be nice, and fairly nearly true, to say that 'from that time forth Eustace was a different boy.' To be strictly accurate, he began to be a different boy. He had relapses. There were many days when he could be very tiresome. But most of those I shall not notice. The cure had begun."[2]

This is a classic story of repentance leading to salvation. Unless we have had this experience, unless we ourselves have been undragoned, there is no hope that we will make any real and lasting progress against the sin in our lives.

As ugly and burdensome as our dragon scales and skins may be, it is often painful for us to part with them. Some of the scales are deeply rooted sins. Some of the dragon scales are layers of defenses we have created and carefully put in place to protect ourselves from God and others. We think that if others knew what we were really like, they could never love us. These scales, too, make us resist change.

Other scales are the nagging bad habits we have formed that make us feel weak and guilty. For these things we take up self-help programs and can through determination occasionally peel off a surface scale or two and feel somewhat better about ourselves. We might lose a few pounds, clean up our language or quit yelling at the kids for a few days.

But what we really need is true repentance, deep penetration and cleansing of our hearts, and we cannot accomplish this on our own. We must have God's help. Even the self-awareness needed to begin the process cannot happen without the grace of God. Only God can show us what we are really like deep down. He alone can lead us through the maze of our scaly defenses and reveal our inner need. And only he can begin in us the healing that brings new life.

Paul writes, "Godly sorrow brings repentance that leads to

salvation and leaves no regret" (2 Cor 7:10). We can praise and thank God in joy when he pierces our hearts and reveals to us the depth of our dragonness. It is the first step toward authentic change. Seeing ourselves as we really are and feeling truly sorry for our sinfulness is the "godly sorrow" that brings genuine repentance. This is a great gift and blessing from God.

True repentance is painful. But without it we can never be free from the burden of our dragonness. God guides us into repentance and seals our turning from sin with a new heart in the Spirit and a new confidence in Christ. A marvelous line from "Amazing Grace" sums up the process beautifully, " 'twas grace that taught my heart to fear, and grace my fears relieved." God's grace reveals our deep need for Christ. And God's grace blesses us with the love and forgiveness that satisfies our need. This is what it means to be set free in Christ.

Several years ago I heard Bob Sheffield of The Navigators tell a moving story that pictured for me the essence of what it means to receive God's forgiveness. Before he became a Christian, Bob played professional hockey in Canada. He was tough, loved to fight and found himself in jail one night after a barroom brawl. Later, Bob and his wife became Christians through The Navigator's outreach ministry. They grew in their newfound faith and accepted a temporary assignment with The Navigators in Christian ministry in the States.

Bob had to apply for landed immigrant status which would allow him and his wife to continue in ministry in the United States. But because he had a criminal record, his request was denied. Fortunately for the Sheffields, their daughter had been born in the U.S., and this worked in their favor. This loophole allowed them to receive the visa they needed to continue their work in the United States.

It was a troubling experience for the Sheffields. Bob realized that they would have this same problem every time The Navigators assigned them to a new ministry in another country.

After much thought and prayer, they decided to apply in Canada for what is called the "Queen's Pardon." A thorough investigation was conducted. The pardon was granted. Bob Sheffield received the following notice in the mail:

> Whereas we have since been implored on behalf of the said Robert Jones Sheffield to extend a pardon to him in respect to the convictions against him, and whereas the solicitor general here submitted a report to us, now know ye therefore, having taken these things into consideration, that we are willing to extend the royal clemency on him, the said Robert J. Sheffield, we have pardoned, remitted and released him of and from the said convictions, and of and from all and every penalty to which he was liable in pursuance thereof.[3]

On any document from that time forward on which Bob was asked if he had a criminal record, he could honestly answer no. What the pardon meant was that he had been released from any possible punishment that could come from the crimes he had committed, and the record of the crimes themselves had been completely erased. When his fingerprints go to the Canadian Mounted Police and they run them through the computer, the printout comes back reading, "No record."

This is the kind of pardon we have in Jesus Christ. When we have received forgiveness, we are set free from any penalty or possible punishment that was due us according to our crimes against God. When Satan requests from the heavenly computer our list of sins punishable by eternal death, it will always print out, "No record. Pardoned by the blood of Christ."

We have been undragoned. We have seen the truth about us, and that truth has moved us to godly sorrow. Because we have repented and believed in the saving grace of Christ, every one of our sins has been erased. Every punishment due to us has been cancelled. When we deserve nothing more than to be blotted out of existence because of our selfishness and sin, God looks to us with grace and mercy and calls us to himself in love.

This is truly Good News.

The Difference Salvation Makes

What does it mean to be saved? How does our salvation in Christ help us now in our struggle with temptation? Does it mean that we are no longer tempted? Are we instantly perfected? Or is there still some fight left in the "old man"? What does God expect from us now? And how has he promised to help us to become everything we were meant to be?

The blessings of God in salvation are boundless. Paul touches on many of the key realities in Romans 5:1-11. Salvation brings peace with God, access to God's grace in which we now stand, hope of realizing the glory intended for us, true development of character leading to strength and endurance in suffering, love empowered by the Holy Spirit as a new motivation for life, an ongoing experience of the risen Christ's sovereign care in our daily lives and the sustained joy of living fully in God. The grace, love, hope, power and joy of God fill us and strengthen us for Christian living in the world.

These are beautiful realities. Everything Paul presents in this passage is true. All of these spiritual experiences are ours in Christ. But nowhere in this passage or in any other are we promised instant perfection. If we were immediately made perfect when we gave our lives to Christ, there would be no need to go on living. It is living out our lives in Christ in the context of the world that strengthens and matures us in the faith. Becoming a Christian is only the first step. As Lewis said of Eustace, he "began to be a different boy." As we enter into life with Christ, the cure has just begun.

If we do not grasp the fact that we are not instantly perfected, we could be in for a difficult but unnecessary struggle. A verse like Romans 6:6 can get us off track. The Revised Standard Version reads, "We know that our old self was crucified with him so that the sinful body might be destroyed, and we might no longer be enslaved to sin." The key term here is *destroyed*. When we read that our old self has been destroyed, we think obliterated, annihilated, put out of existence. The tension this creates for us is that this is simply not what we experience after crossing over into the kingdom of Christ. We are still tempted, and the struggle to resist sin remains. How could this be if our old man was annihilated in the salvation process?

If it is true that my old self is obliterated as this verse apparently suggests, and it is also true that I still struggle with sin, then I am forced to draw conclusions that are unhealthy to my progress as a Christian. First, I might doubt my salvation. The Bible says my old man was destroyed. But I still struggle with sin. Therefore, I must not really be a Christian. Or I might be tempted to lie about my experience, boasting of my deliverance from every temptation and sin, and secretly hoping that no one ever asks my wife if my claims are true. Third, I might distrust God's Word. If the Bible says I should be dead to sin but the possibilities of sin still intrigue me, then the Bible must not be trustworthy.

A better translation of the Greek word *katargete*, which the Revised Standard Version translates "destroyed," is found in the New International Version of the Bible as "rendered powerless." This is more accurate and a great help as well. What the verse is actually saying is that the ultimate power of the old self has been broken by the resurrection power of Jesus Christ.

Once I could not help myself from sinning, but now that I know Christ, I do not have to sin as I did before. It is not that I am dead to sin, like a dead body is completely unresponsive to outside stimulation. But the power of sin to dominate my life has been crushed by the cross of Christ. I can now make true progress with God. I am set free to make real headway against the sin in my life.

Yet my old self hangs on after conversion. It is like an old injury that plagues the body after healing has taken place.

Once when I was riding home from work on my motorcycle, a car ran a stop sign and hit me broadside going 35 mph. After taking the force of the impact on my right leg, I went up over the top of the car and landed on my head in the street. Fortunately I had on a good helmet, and I did not suffer a head injury. But my smashed ankle put me out of commission for a long time. I have since returned to all my normal activities, but the old injury still bothers me from time to time. I have occasional pains in the bone or muscle, and the leg still swells when I have been on it too long and slows me down a bit. But now that I am healed, the old injury no longer has the power to control my life as it did.

This is the way it is with the old man. He is still there, bothering me from time to time, reminding me of my former injury. But now that I have been healed, it is my new health rather than my injury that dominates my life.

This is the interesting thing about God's healing. When he heals, he leaves the broken thing in place. Instead of fixing the broken thing, he brings his power through the Holy Spirit to overpower the brokenness. The balance of power has shifted in our spiritual lives. God does not remove the boulders from the rapids of life; he raises the level of the water.

The point of all this is that Christians do sin. Paul shares in Romans 7:22-25 his personal struggle with temptation. The actions of the twelve apostles during the time that Christ was taken and right after the resurrection show their sins of faithlessness, denial, pessimism and lack of loyalty. And the apostle John writes in a general letter to Christians, "If we claim to be without sin, we deceive ourselves and the truth is not in us" (1 Jn 1:8).

Christians will continue to fight temptation. It is a lifelong battle. The goal for our lives is clear. Peter writes, "As obedient children, do not conform to the evil desires you had when you

lived in ignorance. But just as he who called you is holy, so be
holy in all you do; for it is written: 'Be holy, because I am holy' "
(1 Pet 1:14-16).

God's goal for us is holiness. But what method will he use?
If we are not blessed with instant spiritual perfection, then how
are we to move on toward holiness in God?

Sanctification by Grace

Most of us who have sought Christ have done so because we
have realized we are powerless to save ourselves, that we need
help from outside ourselves to deal with the problem of our
deep-seated sin. We have tried to scrape off a few scales and
have managed to peel away a surface skin or two. But eventually
we realize that the problem is deeper than we can manage. And
so in faith we throw ourselves on the mercy of God.

The next step, though, we do not seem to have down as well.
We thank God for our salvation. Now we see the goal of holy
living ahead. We set out to obtain the goal for Christ. The
problem is, we appear to believe that for the most part our
spiritual growth to maturity still depends wholly on us.

We start with the disciplines of the Christian faith—Bible
study, prayer, Scripture memory. We take on many new programs, attend more classes and support groups, find numerous
places to serve Christ with our lives. But before we know it, we
are out of gas, the edge is off our disciplines, our schedule has
worn us out, and we hear ourselves talking in our support
groups more and more about our failures and less and less
about the joy of living the Christian life. Yet, perhaps this is a
good experience for us. If we come out of it realizing that we
are no better at sanctifying ourselves than we are at saving
ourselves, all is not lost.

God wants holiness to be the mark of our lives. This is God's
vision for us. Before the creation of the world, he saw us holy
in Christ. Paul makes this clear in Ephesians when he writes,

"For he chose us in him (Christ) before the creation of the world to be holy and blameless in his sight" (Eph 1:4). It is important to see that trying to make ourselves holy by continuing to peel off scales and skins will get us about as far as trying to save ourselves by the same method.

The beginning of holiness for us does not lie first in our determined effort to clean up our lives. The road to holiness always begins with submission to God as the prime mover in the sanctifying process. Our highest priority is our relationship with Christ. We commit and recommit ourselves to being willingly responsive in obedience to the call and movement of his Holy Spirit in our lives. We cannot make ourselves holy. What we can do is to learn how to cooperate more completely with the Holy Spirit, and to give ourselves to God according to his timing for our progress. It is a hard job making us holy. But God will have his way. We can count on that.

In one important sense, everything we have been saying about holiness is already a reality in our lives. Holiness is really a done deal. Jesus has already accomplished our righteousness through his sinless life and his sacrificial death on our behalf. 1 John 5:3-5 reads: "This is love for God: to obey his commands. And his commands are not burdensome, for everyone born of God has overcome the world. This is the victory that has overcome the world, even our faith." If we have believed in Christ, we have already overcome the world. Holiness is a present inward reality toward which we are gradually being transformed.

Grasping this truth will change forever how we see God working in our lives to bring about the transformed character he desires. He has already accomplished holiness in us through the death of his son, Jesus. This is God's way of taking the pressure off and letting us grow at a natural rate. It is like being granted a university degree *cum laude* the first day of your freshman year. You have already graduated with highest honors. No need to bite your nails, to worry, to get totally stressed out. No need to stay up late cramming for tests. Now you can really learn. You are set free to develop at your best pace.

God has accomplished righteousness through grace. Now we can live and move in that reality, working in the power of the Spirit toward realizing in our lives what has already been accomplished in Christ. "His commands are not burdensome," John writes. We are supposed to enjoy the freedom of growing in Christ without the pressures of constant guilt, low self-esteem and the frustration of unreal perfectionism. This is the healthy way God has provided for our lifelong growth toward holiness.

In a letter to a struggling friend C. S. Lewis wrote:

I know all about the despair of overcoming chronic temptations. It is not serious, provided self-offended petulance, annoyance at breaking records, impatience etc. don't get the upper hand. No amount of falls will really undo us if we keep on picking ourselves up each time. We shall of course be v. muddy and tattered children by the time we reach home. But the bathrooms are all ready, the towels put out, and the clean clothes in the airing cupboard. The only fatal thing is to lose one's temper and give it up. It is when we notice the dirt that God is most present in us; it is the v. sign of his presence.[4]

All of us have besetting sins that plague us. We become concerned with our lack of progress. The danger here lies in the possibility that we might be tricked into doubting the authenticity of our relationship with Christ on the basis of the fact that we struggle with sin. The truth is, the struggle itself is proof that God is close to us. Our sensitivity to sin is a gift of God's Spirit. It is a sign of our salvation. There would be no inner battle if we were truly lost. Only when we can sin without remorse, with no experience of inner tension, only when sin has become easy for us are we in real danger. Then we must fall down and beg God to enter our lives afresh.

What Can We Do?

If God is at work to purify us and build us into the men he wants us to be, how can we cooperate with his important work?

First, we can learn how to listen better to God and be wiser about our choices in obedience. If God wants to build your character, why not ask him what he's working on now. Instead of making all your own plans and driving ahead to do things your way, spend more quality time with God and train your ear to hear him. This way you will be more able to concentrate your efforts at the same place that God is focusing his life-changing, resurrection power in your life. If we can learn to listen better to God, we will be more responsive to his step-by-step process of building holiness into our lives.

We can also be more patient with ourselves and even more patient with God. We get nowhere by trying to do too much too quickly and then crashing each time we get out ahead of God. It is good when you are going to begin a serious diet-and-exercise program to let your personal physician advise you. If you develop the program on your own, without understanding exactly what you need, you will probably waste a lot of time and energy and never really get where you need to go. Sometimes we take on too much too quickly and then give up in discouragement. God knows what we really need and the steps it will take to get us there. Be satisfied to work more steadily according to God's timing and you will see real progress over time. We can learn to be more responsive to God without losing patience with ourselves. God would want us to relax more and depend more fully on his guidance, wisdom, power and grace.

The key to our ability to live as free men will be whether we can internalize fully that we are forgiven, that God loves us even when we fail, and that our growth toward holiness is in God's loving and sovereign hands. Unless we can accept that both salvation and sanctification are by grace, our striving will always lead to frustration, anxiety and eventual despair, for we will be returning again and again to the hopeless task of trying to earn God's love. This is and always has been an impossible possibility. Jesus died on the cross to free us from the cycle of failure and despair that marks all human attempts to achieve righteousness.

God wants us to learn obedience and experience the joy and freedom that submission to Christ can bring. This can only be accomplished by living daily in Christ, learning from our successes and from our mistakes and failures. God's blessing of forgiveness gives us new beginnings in him. So it is that we progress in the Christian faith and as Peter says, "grow in the grace and knowledge of our Lord and Savior Jesus Christ" (2 Pet 3:18). True joy cannot be had in any other way.

We would do well to remember that God has built into his design for us a normal duration of time for our earthly training in righteousness. He gives us no less than a lifetime. It is good to keep this in mind, otherwise we will lose patience with ourselves and try to do too much too quickly. Real and lasting change always takes time. There is no quick fix with God.

A good chef knows what a long soak in a fine marinade will do for a tough piece of meat. There is no way to slap on a glaze at the last second and get the same fine result. This is God's way with us. We soak in the marinade of his grace for a lifetime, and there is simply no way to rush the process without ruining the meat.

A lifetime of soaking in the marinade of God's grace can transform even the toughest sinner into a heavenly delicacy.

Questions for Groups and Individuals

1. Look through the table of contents. Six of the chapters address particular temptations. Which of these are you most interested in reading? Why?

2. The author uses the metaphor of drowning in a swift current to describe his personal struggle with temptation. (pp. 15-16) Does this picture fit your experience? If not, how would you describe your experience? Explain.

3. The author suggests that temptations to sin are more pervasive and

harder to handle today than they were for earlier generations. (p. 17) Do you agree? What are various reasons that this might be true?

4. This chapter points out how important repentance is to being saved and set free from our sins. (p. 20) Define and discuss repentance.

5. To illustrate how a sinner experiences repentance, the author uses an incident from the life of Eustace in *The Voyage of the Dawn Treader*. (pp. 19-20) Describe your reaction to this story.

6. The author says that in our eagerness to grow in our Christian lives we will sometimes adopt a number of spiritual disciplines that turn out to be only partially effective. (p. 26) Describe experiences you have had with personal spiritual disciplines.

What do you think makes the difference between spiritual disciplines "working" or "failing"? What is the central point the author is making in this area?

7. We are saved by God's grace and do not have to work our way to heaven. Nevertheless, we, like Paul, feel the desire to "press on to take hold of that for which Christ Jesus took hold of [us]" (Phil 3:12). What is the chief thing that motivates you to struggle against sin and press on toward holiness?

8. Describe one way in which this chapter has comforted you.

2/THE TEMPTATION TO BE MACHO

Men lust, but they know not what for;
They wander, and lose track of the goal;
They fight and compete, but they forget the prize;
They spread seed, but spurn the seasons of growth;
They chase power and glory, but miss the meaning of life.
GEORGE GILDER

*T*he weekend was one of the most powerful and uplifting I had ever experienced.

It was a Sunday morning in mid-October. We were finishing our leadership retreat with worship and communion. I sat in a large circle of elders and other staff on the deck of a rustic mountain lodge. The crisp air and intense high altitude sunlight heightened the awesome spiritual experience we were sharing. I was thrilled by the jagged, immense, frozen peaks that rose up out of the valley and formed Berthoud Pass, white and glistening about ten miles to the south. The valley leading up to the pass was a vast dark green blanket of mountain pines.

We sang and prayed and served communion to one another. Then it was time to reflect and share together what the weekend had meant to each of us. I went first. I knew that God had been speaking to me. The elders and staff listened as I told of my renewed thankfulness for the love and generosity of my wife, Judie, and our kids. The most important personal insight I had gained from the weekend was the realization that I spend so much of my time with those outside of my family that I often have nothing left for the ones I should be serving first and best.

I told how Judie and the kids support me in my work; even my younger boys often say, when I have been out several nights in a row: "That's all right, Dad. We know how important this is. We'll be fine." And I started to cry. I was deeply moved by the reality of my family's love for me and for God and his work. And I was ashamed that I had often misused their generous love to take on more speaking than is appropriate, more teaching than I can handle, more meetings than anyone should ever have to attend. I was also grateful to God for his goodness in protecting my family during times when I had been selfish and unwise.

I could not speak. I cried openly and uncontrollably. I could not get the right words out. After a pause that was probably not as long as it seemed, I was finally able to blurt out a confession and asked the others for support in prayer.

I was embarrassed. If I had known that I was about to break down, I probably would not have shared. After another period of silence, some of the others began talking about what the weekend had meant to them. The sharing touched on one topic, then another. None of the others in the circle was moved to tears.

It was then that I began to experience what I think is typical for men in our day. I became concerned about the fact that I had lost control of myself in a public setting. What did the others think of me? I had been a visible leader at the retreat. I was surrounded by strong and committed men and women. Not one of them was crying. But I had broken down in front of them all, blubbering like a baby.

The inner dialog became so strong that I retreated into my

thoughts and psychologically isolated myself from the group for several minutes. Then I heard our pastor begin thanking the elders warmly for their support of him through a difficult year. He talked about losing his father and mother from separate illnesses only months apart. He described what it was like to have to sell the farm in Pennsylvania that had been in the family for generations. Then he went on to talk of the death of his grandfather and a favorite aunt, all in this same year. And on the day of Grandfather's funeral, the faithful old family dog was run over and killed in the road near the house.

As Warren retold the story of his pain-filled year, he too started to cry. He is one of the strongest men I've known. He can carry a great deal. But he, too, was crying openly as I myself had done just minutes before. I realized then what a beautiful thing this was. Observing his willingness to suffer transparently, to let others care about him and for him, cut through all the shallow thoughts that had filled my mind. I knew in no uncertain terms what it meant to be a real man.

Rather than looking down on my pastor and friend for sharing tears of grief with us, I saw that authentic openness is a courageous style in our day. Nothing could be more manly. I thanked God for leading us into the more rewarding realities of genuine community in Christ. It is a truly beautiful thing to be able to feel and live life at the deeper levels, to be free to express real emotions, and to share these realities with others who care too much to judge.

Our goal as Christian men should be to model genuine personal openness and to promote and accept more openness in our churches. This will help free us and other men to be real and whole, instead of handicapped by a world view that leads to an artificial and trivial masculinity.

The Male Cover-Up
Why do we have to be macho? What is wrong with having real

emotions? What is behind our feelings that we have to look and act like supermen in order to be respected or effective? What will free us from our felt need to present to others an external impression that belies the real feelings we carry within?

The machismo image we men tend to project is a behavioral response rooted both in cultural tendencies that are taught and in psychological realities peculiar to men. Society has made little headway toward freeing men to experience and express a broad and healthy range of emotions. Young boys are still teased if they cry. They learn early that being a real man means hiding their feelings.

Even modern women contribute to this cultural tendency. The women's liberation movement lives today in a strange and ironic tension regarding this issue. For years liberated women have promoted the free show of emotion for men. But it is often the liberated woman who is angriest when she cannot control her emotions in public.

A Colorado congresswoman who everyone thought would run for president in the 1988 election announced in the fall of 1987 that she could not find a way to run. When she made the announcement, she broke down in tears and welcomed a hug of encouragement from her husband. Her natural show of emotion was criticized as weakness in Denver papers by women leaders in the community, those same women who have for years been telling us all that it is healthy for men to cry. Sadly, our culture still promotes hiding our emotional side as a strength, and sees public displays of emotion as a sign of weakness.

Young men growing up in America also catch on quickly that physical expressions of caring and friendship between women are normal and accepted, but physical touch between men can be social suicide. Any touch between men in our day more expressive than a handshake raises the usually unwarranted suggestion of sexual intimacy, homosexuality. Crude jokes and cruel remarks continue to breathe life into this irrational taboo among boys and men.

At a college retreat I attended recently as a speaker we were asked by the program leader to form several lines. We all expected to be asked to rub each other's backs. He asked us instead to do a voice-box rub of the person in front of us. I was amazed at how uncomfortable many of the young men were to have to touch another man's throat and neck. The football player in front of me could not stand to have me touch his skin and asked me not to. I fear that too many fathers today still hug and hold their daughters but only box and wrestle with their sons. We are damaged by this kind of socialization.

Men today are taught to compete, that winning is to be sought at the expense of all else, human or divine. Men are taught to be independent. To need others is a sign of weakness. Men are taught to be concerned with the goal and task at hand, that making progress on or accomplishing some project is more important than developing a relationship. Often when I have met a man in our congregation for lunch at my request, he is confused to find that I had no agenda for our meeting, that I simply wanted to get to know him better. Men are taught not to ask for help. Asking for help is also a sign of weakness. This trait is humorously portrayed in the common male tendency of driving around lost for hours while refusing the entire time to stop and ask directions.

In *Men: A Book for Women*, these cultural tendencies are summed up this way:

He shall not cry.

He shall not display weakness.

He shall not need affection or gentleness or warmth.

He shall comfort but not desire comforting.

He shall be needed but not need.

He shall touch but not be touched.

He shall be steel not flesh.

He shall be inviolate in his manhood.

He shall stand alone.[1]

These cultural expectations are powerful enough in themselves to effectively determine much of a man's behavior, but they become even more influential in the development of male personality when they are driven by a fragile male ego and emotional insecurity.

It does not take an expert to recognize when someone is suffering an identity crisis. Most of us know from experience the common cover-up behaviors that signal insecurity. Insecure people are often the ones who mask their true inner emotional reality by coming on strong, trying to maintain control by dominating those around them through power and intimidation. They live and work in impervious psychological shells that hold others at a safe distance. They are never wrong and will go to great lengths to show how something or someone else is always at fault. They will not welcome dialog that suggests that they may need help to change or improve. The behaviors are a dead giveaway. Such a person is locked in an agonizing inner struggle. These behaviors are in varying degrees common in most men.

A peacock raises its tail feathers to scare off attackers. It is a behavior meant to disguise weakness and vulnerability. A turtle retreats into the dense defense of its shell. Men often behave like the peacock or the turtle. If we are in danger of being found out, we will fan our achievements and wield a display of power, or we will retreat into our impenetrable fortresses. Either way our manly image remains intact. We are proud creatures.

George Gilder in *Men and Marriage* argues convincingly that male insecurity is rooted in the sexual differences between men and women.[2] It is almost as if men were behind the door when God gave out the deeper gifts of human sexuality. A man's sexuality is shallow and trivial when compared with a woman's.

Aside from the necessity of planting a seed during intercourse, a man has nothing given to him to which he can point to measure his inherent worth as an individual. And because his sense of masculinity is tied to his ability to perform sexual intercourse, his sexual identity is fragile and only tentatively in place. A man is extremely vulnerable here because his sexuality is dependent upon successful performance. Fear of impotency is profoundly real and operative in the male psyche.

In bold contrast, the woman's sexual nature is multifaceted and has real and long-term significance. Intercourse is only one of many significant sexual realities that make up her life and sexual identity. She knows that she holds within her biological and sexual nature the key to the perpetuation of human community. Her womb and monthly cycle remind her that she can become pregnant, carry and birth a child. Her breasts are symbolic of her central and powerful role of nurturing the children she brings into the world. A woman has been given by nature the dominant role in birthing and raising children. Her role as nurturer positions her to have the greatest and most lasting influence on the quality of character we find in her children. These powerful and ultimately significant acts are hers and hers alone unless she allows her man to share in them. The woman plays, without question, the lead role in the most important drama known to humankind, the perpetuation of human community.

Compared to women, men are conspicuously dispensable. A man cannot find security in his sexuality, as the woman can, because the whole of his sexuality is dependent upon the successful achievement of a single, almost superfluous, act. Men have no given identity, no solid ground or base of significance on which to rest. Margaret Mead has written, "The central problem of every society is to define appropriate roles for the men."[3]

The modern sperm bank with *in vitro* fertilization and, even more devastating, advances in cloning techniques which promise to make it possible for women to have offspring who are clones of themselves (this requires nothing from the man, just a cell, an egg and the womb of a woman) symbolize the fact that men are increasingly becoming a kind of throw-away commodity in our throw-away culture.[4]

So men turn to their functional roles to authenticate themselves, to try to gain a sense of identity. For years men were able to hide behind their jobs and at least keep up appearances of self-significance. Women stayed at home and knew little about what their men did in their carefully guarded private worlds of work. Men protected their fragile identities with their lives.

This explains why so many men have problems today with women entering the work world. Men in the past were able to hold a small piece of life that was theirs and theirs alone. At least they provided for their families so there could be a stable home life during the years that the women raised the children. But today women can be and often do choose to be totally independent. And many women are opting for this new autonomous lifestyle. The woman can have a good and rewarding job and raise a family today while choosing to live alone. And she can do all this without having to put up with the added pressures of dealing daily with the ego problems of an insecure modern man.

At a family get-away recently I consoled a young single mother and affirmed her in the good job of parenting she was doing without a husband. She was quick to tell me that life was a lot easier without him. She used to have to do everything she was now doing plus spend a lot of extra time trying to make their difficult relationship work. She said she would rather live alone than have to expend the energy required to keep the family going and her husband feeling good about himself.

Outside a Christian context, men are in trouble. Even if the world of work were still primarily the domain of men, the problem of male insecurity would not go away. Anytime our identity is tied to performance and function, we are in for a struggle. A simple loss of job can do us in. Or the company can take away our project. And, of course, there is always the possibility that we might stop for a second and realize that no matter what we are producing to keep the great machinery of modern technological life on track, our work does not in itself have eternal and ultimate significance. This realization can be devastating if we have poured years of our lives into our jobs without ever stopping to raise the important questions about the value of our work. A brief testimony from the autobiography of the well-known British politician and author Leonard Woolf brings this point home.

> Looking back at the age of eighty-eight over the fifty-seven years of my political work in England, knowing what I aimed at and the results, meditating on the history of Britain and the world since 1914, I see clearly that I achieved practically nothing. The world today and the history of the human ant hill during the last fifty-seven years would be exactly the same as it is if I had played ping pong instead of sitting on committees and writing books and memoranda. I have therefore to make the rather ignominious confession to myself and to anyone who may read this book that I must have in a long life ground through between 150,000 and 200,000 hours of perfectly useless work.[5]

Our work alone cannot achieve for us the inner security we lack and long for as men. Yes, creative work does have value, but our human achievements in and of themselves do not have unquestionable significance and cannot bring us the deep meaning dimensions and secure identity we seek. If we are honest, we must admit that our work lives are hardly more than a steady stream of relatively meaningless activities—sometimes extraordinarily complex and exciting games of Ping-Pong, but Ping-Pong nevertheless.

The Road to Wholeness

It is the secure man who does not have to act macho. A man who has found a sense of identity and purpose does not need to strut like a peacock or hide his vulnerability within a thick, impenetrable shell. Only when a man is delivered from the burden of having to protect himself or prove his adequacy in the public world will he finally be able to live and work in freedom, and give himself away in love.

If I have received Christ, I am truly free. The immediate results of responding to the gospel are several. First, I feel accepted and loved unconditionally. I know I am valued by God. This frees me from having to convince myself or others that I am worth something. If I know I am loved, I can finally accept and then forget about myself and get on with living my life for others. The gospel frees me to love as I have been loved (Lk 10:27).

Second, forgiveness operates in my life, now and in the future (1 Jn 1:8-9). I no longer have to live the perfect life or try to cover up my inadequacies. This frees me to admit that I am often wrong and sometimes fail. It is fine to be a man who is growing and learning. A free man can accept the help and advice of others.

Finally, in the gospel I find for the first time in my life that I have a truly high calling, meaningful work in the Lord that has eternal rather than superficial value (Mt 28:18-20). A man can be a loving servant-leader in his family, helping to teach the truth of God in Christ, modeling a sacrificial lifestyle and extending unconditional love to his wife and children (1 Pet 3:7-11; Eph 5:21-33; 6:4; Deut 6:1-9). He can be a leader in the church, serving with his hands, his heart or his mind (Tit 1:5-9; 1 Tim 3:1-7). He can be a Christian presence in the world, concerned for reaching the world for Christ and a firm defender of right behavior in the marketplace (Mt 5:13-16; Eph 5:11). He can model Christian manhood in all his relationships, reaching out in love and with truth to other men and women who are, without Christ, hopelessly insecure and filled with fear, trapped in the defensive, fruitless and destructive life patterns of our dying culture (Rom 12:1-2, 9-21).

This is how a man's life can have eternal rather than transient significance.

Christian Manhood

What will be the common behaviors of the Christian man, the biblical man, the man set free in Christ through the power of the gospel?

The Christian man is free to be a servant-leader. He no longer depends on his own strength, but on the guidance, wisdom and strength of the Lord. His identity is not dependent on successful achievement, so he is set free to fail without being devastated by failure. He can make decisions. God gives him guidance through his Word and through prayer. And God can even bring good out of difficult circumstances and redeem errors in judgement. This gives the Christian man courage and faith to step out and take measured risks in the Lord's work. He can include others in the decision-making process because he is no longer afraid to admit that he needs the help of others and of God in order to have success. He can affirm and build up those with whom he works because he feels affirmed and accepted in love by God in Christ.

The Christian man is free to be lighthearted. He no longer has to take himself so seriously. God is his refuge. He is set free from having to protect himself, to fear and shield himself from others. He is secure in himself and in his faith. He will not list out his accomplishments like a peacock fanning his tail. His personality will take on a peaceful playfulness that will draw others to him like a magnet. He can laugh at himself. He has no need to put others down.

The Christian man is free to interact with others. He is relational.

He is a thoughtful neighbor and a congenial host. Once he hid himself from others, but now he is free to share himself openly. He will talk with his wife. He will talk with his children. He will not talk *at them,* but with them, listening to those he loves. He will not have to have all the right answers. He will enjoy entering into the deeper-meaning dimensions of the lives of those around him. He is no longer interested in telling others how important he is. He is now more interested in hearing about *their* joys, *their* needs, *their* hopes, *their* dreams. The Christian man is able to talk with others about his needs and to ask for help. He knows that it is his willingness to open his life to others that creates possibilities for himself and others to grow, receive healing and move on toward maturity in Christ. The Christian man will give and receive friendship.

The Christian man is free to be tender. He no longer has to analyze everything objectively and express himself without feeling. He is now strong enough to be gentle. He will touch and hold and kiss his children, sons and daughters, as Jesus held the children of his day and loved them. He will affirm others with words of truth and love and be generous with hugs and other physical expressions of encouragement. He will let others affirm and love him. He can laugh and cry like Jesus did with those he loves.

The Christian man is free to forgive. He will forgive others quickly and with a generous spirit as he has been forgiven by God. A redeemed sinner, and in process himself, he can sympathize and empathize with the struggles of others.

The Christian man is free to stand for righteousness. He will influence his world by courageously speaking the truth and acting on the truth he knows. Once he was too insecure to stand up for what he believed, but now he is secure in Christ's love. He has the courage to expose the fruitless behaviors of darkness and to model the fruitful lifestyle of light, love and truth.

The Christian man is free to be concerned for the world around him.

No longer driven by a need to build external evidences of his worth, he can give himself and his money away. He can work less to build his personal empire, and more to alleviate suffering, hunger and the conditions that lead to distress, disease and death.

The Christian man is free to live in love, joy, peace, patience, kindness, goodness, faithfulness, gentleness and self-control.

But Can We Really Change?

Here it might be good to reread and rethink chapter one. The above listing of some of the marks of authentic Christian manhood is meant to be freeing. But if read in the wrong spirit it could overwhelm us with feelings of failure, guilt or inadequacy. This is the last thing we men need.

It is important to remember above all that we have a lifetime to grow into the mature men God would have us be. These qualities are targets. They are not immediately ours when we become Christians. They are, though, possible for us once we belong to Christ in a way that they were not possible for us before. It will often take years to make notable progress in the areas that are most difficult for us. The difference in Christ, though, is that progress can be made and it is real.

There is hope for us in Christ. The important thing is to take the first step and to follow after it by courageously taking one more step, then another. Do not be discouraged if you cannot improve everything significantly overnight. Real and lasting change takes time.

I remember attending a conference once at which we were asked to draw a diagram that would graphically illustrate our experience of growing in the Christian life. Most of the others represented their growth by a line that rose, dropped sharply, then rose again to a plateau before taking the next deep dive. The more I thought about it, the more I felt that this type of line drawing did not say enough about the patterns of growth

I was experiencing in Christ. The thing that confused and frustrated me about my growth path was that I would have an apparent victory over something, feeling that I had dealt with it and put it behind me, only to find it cropping up again a few months or a year later when I least expected it. I questioned whether I was making any real progress in my Christian walk.

Finally, I penciled the graphic illustration below.

I saw that my Christian growth resembled a steady climb up and around a mountain as I inched my way toward the summit. The mountain has many crevices, cliffs and ledges, problem areas that must be faced. I would work myself through a difficult spot and move on to the next. But eventually, as I circled the mountain, I inevitably returned to the same areas with which I had previously struggled. There I was again dealing with the problem I thought I had licked on the last pass.

This experience of meeting and having to deal repeatedly with familiar battles was the element in my Christian growth that used to discourage me. But when I drew my path up and around the mountain, I came to see my experience in a new light. I realized that each time I return to an area through which I have previously struggled I return at a higher level. God brings us back for a second and third pass because we have more to learn about how to manage that aspect of our lives. But we are moving steadily upward in our growth. We are making progress with God, and over time we will leave some of those crevices, cliffs and ledges behind for good and discover new challenges at the higher elevations.

The higher we climb, the more quickly we will circle the mountain. As we age, our growth accelerates. We face more and more difficulties and are compelled by life's circumstances to continue to reach more deeply into the resources of God. The final growth experience in our climb is, of course, physical death. Our growth will move ahead in quantum leaps as we meet and live through that final and deeply personal transition from this world to the next.

Experience has convinced me that the key to becoming everything God wants us to be as Christian men is to put away our pride, tuck in our external display of fancy-colored feathers, risk squeezing out of our protective shells, admit to ourselves and others that we have a long way to go, and take the first small steps toward lifelong change. God will bless us if we will choose a teachable spirit as our basic disposition in the Lord.

This requires that we allow our wives, our children, our business associates, our brothers and sisters in Christ to share in our deep secret. We are not perfect. We are not together. We are not always strong. We need love. We are often afraid that we are hopelessly behind and might never catch up. We do not know how to get started on the right path. But if we will choose to admit our humanness, God can begin his incredible and miraculous work of remaking us into his image and bringing about in us mature Christian manhood.

In a most practical sense this might mean for some of us honestly admitting that we need outside help to move ahead—counseling with a professional to sort out problems we might be experiencing in our marriages and with our children. Or it may mean, for others of us, joining the most basic Bible study class offered in our church, even though we have given the impression for years that we are really quite far along in the Christian faith. It may mean that we will have to ask others to teach us how to pray or get their advice on other basics of the Christian life. Whatever it is we need to do to take the first step, that is what we should do without concern for our image or ego. This may be the hardest thing for us as men. But it is the only way to move ahead to maturity in Christ.

The Masculine Man
One final and important thing to be said is that we need to resist the temptation today to give in to societal pressures to adopt androgyny as our way of understanding the sexes. We should not give up the important work of trying to understand the distinctives which make us men and women according to God's creative design. Trying to make a definitive case for what is uniquely male and what is uniquely female is a complex and difficult study that has often been shallowly attempted, creating false stereotypes that can be harmful and artificial for both men and women. We are faced with tough questions here. The temptation is to take the easy way out, to say that all roles are interchangeable, that there is nothing different about men and women except the purely biological reality that a woman can have babies and a man cannot.[6] The fact remains that God chose to create and individuate us in this way, as male and female. It is our obligation to try to understand why he made us as he did rather than to blur distinctives or stick our heads in the sands of androgyny.

The practical reality that confronts us is that proper modeling of femininity and masculinity are absolutely essential for the continued health and vitality of both our personal and family lives. It can also be convincingly argued that the health of our future society is at stake in this issue and depends on how well we can keep these distinctions in focus and act them out in appropriate masculine and feminine leadership.[7] We need to remind ourselves constantly that women make the best wives and mothers. Men make the best husbands and fathers. When the images are blurred and biblical sexual realities disdained, the result is that adequacy of personality, emotional balance and wholeness, and healthy self-concepts disappear. Then weakness, insecurity, inability to trust, dependent personalities, emotional illness, paranoia, violent pathologies and sexual deviancy threaten to become the norm rather than the exception for future generations.[8]

Men, there is a difference between being masculine and being macho. Masculinity is our healthy expression of the uniqueness of being created a man in God's design. The behaviors of the macho man are instead unhealthy expressions of the stereotypes of masculinity lived out in their most extreme forms. The macho man perverts true masculinity. He pretends to be strong by acting aggressively and creating about himself an image of power, both of which mask the deeper reality of insecurity within. The truly masculine man knows who he is in God and enjoys a healthy integration of his emotional, intellectual, physical and spiritual nature. This wholeness comes from knowing and responding to the truth that he is fully loved and accepted in Christ. This masculine man in Christ is truly set free to become all he is meant to be.

The macho man lives out an image of manhood that emphasizes only one small part of what it means to be male. He pretends that it is possible to live life with a constant erection. But our physical genital reality reminds us that we are only sometimes hard. Most of the time we are soft. The majority of our lives is lived out as penis, not erected phallus, and this is normal and proper for men.[9] Think of what it would be like in actuality if we had to live the whole of our lives with an erection. This is a grotesque image. Yet it is the kind of masculine image many macho men attempt to convey through their personalities as they relate to those around them.

It is far healthier and more productive to recognize and celebrate the broader dimensions of our masculinity modeled for us most completely by the man Jesus, our loving Lord. Learn to be a strong man according to the biblical image of masculine strength found in him. Study his masculinity. Read through the Gospels and learn from his model of gentle strength. Demonstrate with your life that a man's strength is not rooted in violent aggression or in an obsession with worldly power, but in the Godlike power of sacrificial love.

A man is not weak, but strong, when he wisely chooses to live the predominant portion of his life with his sword in its sheath. This is not a man feminized. This is a masculine man who has given up the false God of proud machismo and has delivered his complex and diverse masculine personality into the hands of God to be shaped by the demands of love.

Questions for Groups and Individuals

1. Does the term *macho* have good or bad connotations for you?

Visualize a man whom you would call "macho." How would you describe him?

2. The author theorizes that male insecurity is linked to the fact that women may have a stronger natural base of identity and self-worth than men. (p. 39) Does this agree with your experience? Why or why not?

3. The author suggests that men trying to maintain their macho images are apt to behave either like peacocks—showing off their achievements— or like turtles—retreating into impenetrable shells. (p. 42) Which behavior do you think is more typical of you?

4. How can having a personal relationship with Christ free a man from the need to act macho?

5. Think through the marks that typify the man who has been set free in

Christ. In which area have you seen growth in yourself? In which area do you feel growth is still needed?

6. What do you think would be involved in bringing up your sons to be men without teaching them to be macho?

3/THE TEMPTATION OF SEXUAL LUST

Lust is the ape that gibbers in our loins.
Tame him as we will by day, he rages all the wilder
in our dreams by night. Just when we think we're safe from
him, he raises up his ugly head and smirks, and there's
no river in the world flows cold and strong enough
to strike him down. Almighty God, why dost thou
deck men out with such a loathsome toy?

FREDERICK BUECHNER

I was moved by reading an article a few years ago that was a Christian leader's confession of sexual obsession. He told of his growing fascination with sex. As a young man, he was drawn to the pictures in *Playboy* magazine. Later, achieving some prominence as a traveling conference speaker, he gave in frequently to the temptation to visit adult bookstores in cities where he was invited to speak. Then he tried sex clubs with nude dancers. He was a voyeur and a self-stimulator. His obsession was powerful. It dominated his life. It skewed his perception of reality. He told how it did not seem wrong to him to reward himself for good work done on writing next Sunday's sermon by taking a well-deserved break to look at nude women in his secret stash of magazines. He had the courage to reveal in detail his powerful personal struggle.[1]

There is not a man alive that does not understand the immense power of the male sexual drive. Just a glimpse of a nipple is usually enough to stop a man in his tracks and captivate his attention. I empathized with the struggle of this pastor. It was most encouraging to read about his path to recovery, God's work of deliverance that helped him to begin to gain control. Then, in a recent article written by the same man, five years after the first, he tells of how God continues to bring strength and help to overpower the obsession. There is always hope in God.[2]

Sex has enormous power. It is power to create and sustain community. Power to live in love. Power to know another deeply. Power to express the image of God. It is both a gift and a profound blessing from the Lord of love.

If perverted, sex is a power that destroys. It holds men captive. Turns quickly to an obsession. Burns with lust. It demeans human beings, reducing them to things to be used, abused and discarded. Held in its bondage, otherwise reasonable men will lie to themselves and others, turn their hearts and minds away from God, leave their wives and the children they love, and choose to live in tension, guilt and shame, all for the promise of tasting again the brief, pulsing current of its seductive pleasure.

How can we manage its power? How can we keep from being seduced? How are we to live out our sexuality in ways that are pleasing to God?

Sex Trivialized: The Modern View

Key principles in God's design for sexuality cannot be violated without causing great harm. For one thing, sex can never be the meaning of life. The powerful illusion that has cast its spell over the entire secular culture today is that sex is a magical experience which will bring into our lives the true intimacy we desire.

It is a lie. Sex which ignores God will only increase our loneliness. But there is a seductive power in the illusion. The physical sensations of sex are very real and strongly suggest intimacy, warmth, deep relating. The emotions involved in casual sex make people feel like they have engaged in something authentic. But beneath the physical sensations there is nothing.

The paradox in the sexual revolution is that what is really wanted and needed and sought after by men and women cannot be achieved in the experience of free sex. True intimacy and irresponsible sex are a contradiction. Free sex by definition must be temporary, anonymous, self-centered. Otherwise it would not be free.

The propaganda promises that irresponsible sex will somehow bring warmth, caring, genuine intimacy. But the images of the sexual revolution betray a different reality. The pictures are always inhuman and unreal. The magazine photographs are touched up, unknown bodies without personality. The bodies feed our fantasies but not our souls. If we indulge ourselves we will only be hungrier than before. Only a real woman and a real relationship can bring us the genuine joy of true intimacy.

Our insecurity and emptiness feed the power of the images. We see in the photographs and mental fantasies of our secret women an opportunity to be for a brief moment sex kings without the tension of fear of impotency, failure in relationship, failure of love. The dark power of physical sex seduces our minds through our emotions. If we stop for a moment and engage our reason to think clearly about what we are doing, we see the illusion for what it really is—a cheap lie. Authentic relationship is impossible without responsible commitment. The physical experience of sex alone will never bring the wholeness and integration for which we deeply long. As J. R. Braun puts it, "Orgasm can never be the meaning of life."[3]

Sex today has been reduced to a physical, genital reality. It is a much-sought-after physical sensation, an intense physical pleasure. It is like the thrill of a roller coaster and the relaxation of a hot tub rolled into one. The evil in this contemporary, trivialized view is that once the reduction is made, many things that are entirely outside of God's holy intent for our sexual lives become possible and even seem to make sense.

If sex is nothing more than a physical experience, a bodily pleasure, if it is just a kind of physical tension and release like scratching an itch, then what difference could it make how one has the experience? Why not achieve the release of sexual tension yourself? Or why not have sex with a machine? If sex is just a good feeling like a massage, why not experience it with someone of the same sex? Why not outside of marriage? Why not with your own daughter?

I have read about establishments for gay men in San Francisco where a man can enter a stall and insert his genitals through an opening in the wall. There he can have a sex act performed on him without even seeing the person on the other side. Why not? If sex is just a feeling, what difference does it make how the feeling is achieved? The modern trivialized view of the sexual experience drives us to this kind of perverse pollution.

The movement has left us emotionally bankrupt, has contributed immensely to the destruction of the American family, and threatens to undermine the very foundation of future society. The worldly view of diminished sex is jammed down our throats from every direction. The propaganda is relentless and intense. Television, books, magazines, movies, all claim that genital sex can somehow bring happiness. Our loneliness, confusion, insecurity and disillusionment make us ripe for exploitation. The more we try to solve our problem of loneliness through casual sex, the more lonely we become. Sex outside of the relational dynamics of God's design, cheap sex, is never ever really cheap. Those who buy into it do so at a great price, the destruction of human personality.

Dimensions of Biblical Sexuality

Knowing God's purpose in creating us as sexual beings is essential to our health in this area. If we know the high calling of God for our sexual lives—the arena within which our sexuality operates as a rich gift and blessing from God—it is more likely that we will remain free and focused in our action.

Genesis has much to say about the meaning of our sexuality and God's purpose in creating us as sexual beings. First, our sexuality is rooted in the very nature of God. "Then God said, 'Let us make man in our image, in our likeness.' . . . So God created man in his own image, in the image of God he created him; male and female he created them" (Gen 1:26-27). Human sexuality is reflected in the creation of two and only two—not three or four—different sexual genders. God was deliberate in his choice of making two distinct sexual beings, a man and a woman, not an androgynous combination of genders. By making us in his image, God chose to mirror his personality in us through our sexual identity as men and women.

God saw that it was not good for the man to be alone (Gen 2:18). He created woman to labor with the man to fulfill the dominion mandate to subdue the earth (Gen 1:28). The fact of our maleness and femaleness is a living reminder that we were created to live in loving relationship, in community. God's purpose is clear. "For this reason a man will leave his father and mother and be united to his wife, and the two shall become one flesh" (Gen 2:24). Through the bonding of their physical and spiritual selves in a loving marriage, a man and woman share the most intimate human community possible, which the Bible describes as "one flesh." This helps explain the powerful drive we have to unite with the opposite sex. We were meant for each other.

God has existed from eternity as a loving relationship, the Trinity of Father, Son and Spirit. He desires for us a similar experience of living in a loving relationship. The creative un-

ion of a man and woman as one flesh in marriage is a union
born out of mutual, self-giving love. A marriage that is good in
God's eyes will reflect his model for effective living, responsible,
long-term commitment to a relationship of selfless love. The
sexual union in marriage is a gift given for mutual delight, but
as is true of all of God's great gifts, it is a gift that also carries
with it the responsibility of stewardship.

The Genesis account reveals yet another aspect of God's divine purpose for marriage which reaches beyond the essential
relationship of the two in one. God says to Adam and Eve, "Be
fruitful and increase in number; fill the earth and subdue it"
(Gen 1:28). Sex without the potential for reproduction is in
danger of becoming trivial and void of meaning. I emphasize
strongly that sex is meant to be a wonderful, shared pleasure
for a couple in marriage. Men and women are to enjoy sex as
a celebration of their blessed union under God. But sex which
aims only at realizing an experience of pleasure is less than
God intends. It is always a part of love, at least the love that
originates in God, that longs to reproduce itself, to extend itself
toward others in faithful action. It is significant that God's ultimate act of love toward us was his choice to bring forth a child
into the world. The coming of the Lord of life as a baby in
Bethlehem is a striking paradigm of God's outreaching love.

Biblical sexuality demands accountability to the fact that
physical love expressed between a man and woman in marriage
has the potential for producing offspring. Sexuality cannot be
rightly understood if the notion of procreation is stripped from
it. It is faithful stewardship under God for Christian couples to
think responsibly about choosing to have children. The biblical
ideal for marriage is creative, generative, outreaching in love.
For the Christian couple, having a child is an obedient and
faithful act which recognizes the importance of producing a
godly heritage of Christian children who represent the hope,
love and promise of God for generations to come.

The Genesis account is rich with meaning. We are created in God's image, male and female. We have the high calling as sexual beings to become one flesh in marriage. And as God reached out in love by creating us and incarnating himself into the world as Savior, we are to love as well, acting responsibly through the gift of sex to be fruitful for God and increase the community of faith for the good of the future of his kingdom in the world.

It is time to take a stand. It is not too late to demand for ourselves and for our society a return to the purposes and practices for sexual life defined and commanded by the Word of God. It will not be easy. This fight may be one of the most difficult we will face as Christian men. The dark forces of sex are powerful. Each time we give in—stimulate ourselves through fantasies or voyeurism, become involved in casual sex, or argue for the rightness of physical sex outside of marriage or between partners of the same sex—we participate in the lie. But when we hold out for God in the various areas of our sexual lives, refusing to play the world's games, insisting on behavior we know is right and true, we will realize a deep blessing from God.

There is only one way to enter into the fullness of sexual life God intends for us. It is the way of obedience born of love.

Sexual Addiction

I said that I empathized with the Christian leader's struggle described at the beginning of the chapter. That is because I have dealt with obsessions as well. *Playboy* magazine also intrigued me as a young man.

It was during a family vacation on a small island in Lake of the Woods in Canada that I first learned to masturbate. I was about ten. I smoked my first cigarette on the same vacation and became addicted to smoking. Both addictions became a force in my life for many years to come. But it was not until my late teens and early twenties that the habits began to wear on my psyche. I knew smoking two or three packs of cigarettes a day would very likely kill me, and there was something about continuing to masturbate after marriage that just did not seem right to me even before I was a Christian.

These two obsessions dominated my life and caused me a great deal of mental agony for many years. The smoking habit went first. On the cold, October afternoon that I gave my life to Christ and was baptized in the Mississippi River I prayed that God would take away my addiction to tobacco. On that day God delivered me from my intense smoking habit. I have never smoked another cigarette. That was nineteen years ago. I have no good explanation for why God would choose to answer my prayer and deliver me from my obsession with smoking, but did not seem to hear my often desperate prayers for the strength to stop masturbating.

Shortly after becoming a Christian, I carried several large stacks of my *Playboy* magazines to the alley and threw them in the trash. It was a good first step. But for a man who waited eagerly each month for years to see (not read) the next issue, dumping the magazines was not the end of my personal struggle. Yet, perhaps this act saved me from becoming more obsessed, more possessed with sexual lust. I thank God that I was not compulsively driven to adult bookstores and XXX-rated sex shows like my brother in Christ whose confession I read with great interest and sympathy. Still, as a Christian man, a father, a husband, a teacher, a preacher, a counselor, I lived with the guilt and tension of keeping up an exterior impression of Christian strength and obedience while knowing that I did not have the sexual area of my life under control.

Honestly facing up to a problem is never easy. Rationalization and denial can keep us going for years. Our lies become old friends after a while. They fill the gap between our obsessive behavior and the pain of our repeated failures. They make it possible for us to go on living without being smothered by the guilt.

I told myself that masturbation was normal for all men. It was nothing to be concerned about. After all, the Bible never even mentions the topic, much less naming it as a sin. I also convinced myself that the habit helped me to release sexual energy when I was away from Judie. Otherwise I might be tempted to have an affair. I told myself that masturbating helped me to control premature ejaculation, enhancing the pleasure of our physical sex in marriage. And there were many other compelling rationalizations with some truth to them. Perhaps you can add a few of your own. But the bottom line was that I was never fully persuaded. My habit held me in its spell, and I could not help feeling less than fully God's man.

It took years to get to the point where I really felt I understood many of the personal factors that contributed to my behavior. The important thing is that the Lord did bring me to a place of decision. One morning in prayer I was overwhelmed with a feeling of deep shame. I opened up the area of my sexual habit to the Lord. I had done this before, but for some reason the depth of feeling and reality in repentance and the sense of inner release were penetrating and undeniably real. God would no longer accept the lies that had worked for me before. God helped me to pour out my pain, and then I felt renewed by his love and promise.

I was led to make a covenant with God that morning. It is a vow and promise I intend to keep for life. By God's grace and power I will keep it. I say this humbly because I know my own human frailty. But I say it in faith believing because I know the power of the Spirit to strengthen my weakness. A long time has passed since the morning of my covenant, and I have not returned to my sin.

For me, refusing to engage in the physical act of self-stimulation has helped me to gain control over other related areas of sexual sin. Knowing that I will not gain sexual relief through masturbation, I am less likely to torture myself by staring at attractive women on the street or on the pages of magazines. I do not want to watch films that contain images that can linger and become bothersome. I do not want to engage in lengthy fantasies about real or imagined women. Stopping the physical reality can help immensely to reduce the power of the mental reality.

At the same time, I am not naive. Refusing to give in to the temptation to masturbate is only one small part of the struggle. Controlling the external behavior is not enough for God. Jesus confronted the Pharisees again and again on this issue. They kept the legal tenets of the law with external perfection, but internally they were filled with sin. The legal approach to overcoming our sin will not free us. Jesus said, "You have heard that it was said, 'Do not commit adultery.' But I tell you that anyone who looks at a woman lustfully has already committed adultery with her in his heart" (Mt 5:27-28).

There is only one way to be moral in this new sense. Jesus did not suggest the unhealthy suppression of inner desires as the way to freedom. His answer to our struggle with sin is new birth, an indwelling of the Holy Spirit, the eventual complete transformation of our personalities after his own image. The more we grow in Christlike love, the more we will grow out of our obsession with self. Jesus is not interested in external piety; he wants purity of heart. His love can change our hearts. We can cooperate by choosing obedience moment by moment as we live in him.

Our choices to stop a physical behavior do not automatically quell the intense drive within. But when the external behavior feeds the intensity within, making that determined first step can, with repentance and an honest turning toward God, begin the inner healing.

The sexual temptation is present in my life. Unlike God's

prior work of delivering me from my smoking habit that has left me without even the slightest urge to smoke, sexual temptation is still something I have to guard against daily. It is an ongoing battle, but one in which it is possible to make real headway. The memory of the tension of the old habit is vivid in my mind. I never want to return to the old way. God's peace is too great a blessing to sacrifice for a moment of selfish indulgence.

What's Wrong with Masturbation?

The Bible is practically silent on the topic of self-stimulation. The one passage that might be aimed at the practice (although I know of no other sources that say this) is Matthew 5:27-30. This is the text I've already quoted in which Jesus talks about looking upon a woman with lust and committing adultery in the heart. The unusual aspect is that in the same breath he goes on to say, "If your right eye causes you to sin, gouge it out . . . and if your right hand causes you to sin, cut it off and throw it away." There is hyperbole here, of course, and the verse is not to be taken and acted upon in its most literal sense. The important thing to see is that the connection of the eye and the hand in this context makes a strong suggestion that the practice of masturbation feeds our sinful lust.

Imagine yourself sitting in that crowd. You are listening to Jesus preach. You hear him say that if you look with lust on another woman you have committed adultery in your heart. He tells you that your eye has led you into sin. He tells you that your right hand leads you into sin. If masturbation is an obsession with you, you will certainly hear a condemnation from the Lord.

One of the greatest stumbling blocks for me when I was trying to gain control over this sexual habit was that almost all books that talk about masturbation, Christian and secular, talk of it as a natural occurrence for men and one we should not worry about. I believe instead that although masturbation will

cause you no bodily harm, it can eventually turn to an obsession which greatly affects the way you think about yourself and
the way you interact with others. It is not enough when we
struggle under the burden of something overpowering to say
that we should simply try to forget about it and not feel guilty.
Paul says, "I will not be mastered by anything" (1 Cor. 6:12).
This should be our goal as well. If we find ourselves troubled
and frustrated and feeling ashamed and guilty over our sexual
practice, we should persist in our prayers and seek the freedom
only God can give to gain power over the power of sin.

Rather than helping in controlling sexual drive, masturbation often has the reverse effect of feeding sexual drive. The
person engaged in the behavior is looking at, or looking at
pictures of or imaging, women. He is living out vicariously the
sin of sexual lust. Braun writes: "The masturbator sees in the
sexual fantasy a body for his own gratification rather than a
person he must interact with in Christ. His (or her) goal is not
to create a unity of persons with Christ the mediator, but to
indulge himself. The more he masturbates, the more he learns
to seek his own fulfillment. It is very difficult for the masturbator to move from self-absorption to community."[4] Masturbation
most often increases rather than decreases the sexual drive to
have the other woman, whether the woman is real or imagined.

The point is, the practice can inhibit the development of the
relationship toward which our sexuality aims. John White has
described masturbation as "sex on a desert island." As such, it
diminishes the sexual, physical and mental energy that should
be a resource for the making and keeping of a good and caring
relationship with another.

At the same time I have to turn the question back in your
direction, because like so many areas of concern for Christians,
this is one where there is much debate and difference of opinion. You need to decide the level of harm in your behavior. I
felt strongly that the regularity with which I turned to self-

stimulation was wrong, and I carried guilt and shame that kept me from living at the level I wanted to live with God. I could not put the question aside. Perhaps your feelings and practice are not at all the same as mine.

Remember, too, that I am talking here man to man. You are a mature man dealing on a mature level with this topic. My counsel and help would be very different if I were talking with young people who struggle with intense sexual feelings and have no acceptable sexual outlet. These young men and women need to be encouraged and helped to accept God's unconditional love, grace and forgiveness. This is a topic that should be addressed differently at different levels of maturity. The main question here is whether you are at the point in your development where you want to deal more directly with the problem of sexual temptation.

My intent is to be helpful, not harsh and unforgiving. God forgave me a hundred times or more as I worked through this battle to gain control. He may need to forgive me again. I am not a fool when it comes to recognizing my areas of vulnerability. But I know now what it is like to be free from this agonizing personal struggle. Knowing the spiritual pleasure of this freedom in Christ increases my sense of urgency to hold out for you something better than the mediocrity of a life clouded by this sexual obsession or any other. Accept God's love and forgiveness if you struggle in this area. But have the courage as well to pray that God will keep you dealing honestly with him as you seek his will for your life.

My particular obsession was masturbation. Yours may be something else. Pornography might have a grip on you. Or you may find it difficult to resist nightclubs that feature nude dancers. You may be overpowered by the desire to have a prostitute. You may even secretly desire your own daughter or one of your young daughter's friends.

If the sexual area is a battleground in your life, admit your

weakness and be willing to enter into an accountable relationship with someone you trust before the power of sex destroys
you. Be careful. The sexual area is one in which we are particularly prone to both rationalization and fear of exposure.
This is why it is so important to seek help if you struggle with
sexual addiction. It's too tough to go it alone. We need the
encouragement and accountability we can get from others.
Many churches have now begun groups for men and women
to help deal with addictive behaviors, including sexual addictions. Talk to your pastor. Or share your struggle with a trusted
friend. You may want to consider seeing a Christian counselor
or therapist. There are also good inpatient facilities like the
Carnes Golden Valley Health Center in Minneapolis if you
need more concentrated help to beat sexual addiction. Remember, too, that healing is seldom a single significant event,
but usually occurs with successive changes over a long period
of time. So don't punish yourself if you do not see immense
progress every week.

But don't give up the fight.

What's Wrong with Pornography?

It almost goes without saying that the ugliest aspect of pornography is that those who produce it exploit and dehumanize
those who give themselves to or are forced to be a part of
pornographic media. The use of children in pornographic
materials is particularly disgusting. Many children who appear
in pornographic films and magazines are children who have
been kidnapped or have run away and now need to find a way
to make money on their own. The exploitation and violence
that are a part of this evil industry are well documented.[5]

What is wrong with pornography as it presents sexuality is
that it radically disconnects the sexual experience from its godly
purpose and design (Gen 2:24). Pornography is an entire movement based on the reduction of sexuality I wrote about in ear-

lier paragraphs. The fullness of what God intends for human sexuality, the beautiful bonding of a man and woman in the relationship of one flesh, in the experience the Hebrews expressed as "to know" another in the deepest sense of the word, is diminished to its lowest animal, physical dimension and played upon by the producers of porn.

Pornography plays on our deepest insecurities and fears of failure in relationship. It presents an illusion, an empty promise of relationship, while taking advantage of the fact that the desire that drives the insecure man is to fulfill the fantasy without having to risk the failure of real relationship. The ugly reality in pornography is that it lures men away from true relationship. They become lost souls chasing an illusion, a mirage. The longer they chase the titillating image, the longer they will live empty lives, not able to find and enjoy the deep integration of their personalities with a woman in love, which is the goal of God for our human sexuality.

I have compassion for those who are locked in the grip of pornography. It is a shockingly powerful addiction. The horror of it is that a gift so beautiful and holy as the gift of sex from God can be so utterly and disgustingly perverted.

What's Wrong with Homosexuality?

The argument that homosexuality is just a special form of normal sexuality is untenable from a biblical perspective. Homosexual behavior ignores God's primary purpose and design for sexual life. It denies the pre-eminently important procreative dimension that is the cornerstone of God's intention for human sexuality. All orifices are not created equal in God's design.

Homosexual men and women also confuse the authentic experience of love between good friends by adding a physical sexual element to the relationship which the Bible does not condone. " 'Do not lie with a man as one lies with a woman;

that is detestable'" is God's word from Leviticus 18:22. The Hebrew word *toebah* used here and translated "detestable" means literally something detestable and hated by God (see also Prov 6:16; 11:1). Homosexuality is morally wrong and keeps company with adultery, child sacrifice and bestiality (Lev 18:20-21, 23). The New Testament also prohibits homosexual behavior in Romans 1:26-27, 1 Corinthians 6:9 and 1 Timothy 1:10.

The Romans passage is especially significant because it discusses homosexuality in the broader context of humanity's relationship to God as Paul establishes the guilt of all humans and their need for salvation in Christ. The verses read, "Because of this, God gave them over to shameful lusts. Even their women exchanged natural relations for unnatural ones. In the same way the men also abandoned natural relations with women and were inflamed with lust for one another. Men committed indecent acts with other men, and received in themselves the due penalty for their perversion" (Rom 1:26-27). The larger context for Paul's argument is that all are without excuse before God because they already know that their actions violate the basic character of God. Some repress this knowledge and continue in their sin.

Homosexuality is not just a behavior Christians and Jews disapprove of. Paul argues that it is one of a number of practices which clearly violate the light of God in nature, creation and human conscience (Rom 1:18-20; 2:14-15). This is why it will do no good to argue that Paul was just condemning in this Scripture irresponsible or promiscuous homosexual behavior. It is clearly homosexuality per se that is contrary to nature and to the will and character of God.

It is certainly impossible in this small space to do justice to this complex topic.[6] But it must be said that even though many men and women are drawn more intensely to members of their own sex, this predisposition toward homosexual behavior does not free them from acting responsibly in accord with biblical norms. Alcoholics may be born with a predisposition to drink. They have no part in their orientation toward addiction to alcohol. But just because they are physically and psychologically set up in such a way that they are drawn to alcohol does not mean that they are free from the obligation as a Christian to act responsibly in controlling their behavior.

The man or woman with a homosexual orientation and the single person who has no biblically legitimate outlet for physical sexual expression are in a somewhat similar position of tension. Both are called by God to responsibly control their sexuality, according to biblical teaching in this area. Fornication is not an option.

I know a number of single men and women who struggle with these issues. We pray and work together to achieve what we believe to be right under God. The sexual drive of the single man is often very strong. He wants to find a wife, but he does not find one. The homosexual friend would do anything if he could feel the same attraction for a woman that he now feels for men. The emotional pain in these circumstances is immense. But the church cannot give permission to the single man who cannot find a wife to sleep with any woman he can find. Nor can the church give permission for the homosexual person who feels unable to change his sexual orientation to be sexually active with another man. Both cases require the greatest courage and Christian intentionality for the people involved. And some have told me they find great joy in a celibate lifestyle that frees them to live at peace in the church and in the world without the driving obsession to realize genital physical sex.

Sex and the Single Man

A lot of what is happening among singles in the church today is frightening and disturbing. I was recently on a talk show in

Detroit. The topic was evangelism. A young woman called in and told about the young man who first talked with her about Christ. He invited her to church and to a young singles class. There she heard for the first time good biblical teaching that reflected the love and grace of Christ. She gave her life to the Lord. She expressed deep joy in her testimony.

But what she really wanted to talk to me about was the sexual conduct of the young man who invited her to church. It turned out that he was not really interested in her salvation at all. The invitation to church was apparently his way of initiating a relationship he hoped would satisfy his sexual lust. It was a subtle deception. She—and probably others like her—thought that a young man who would invite her to church would certainly be safe.

Shortly after her initial visit to the church the man called her for a date. She had a number of things she felt she wanted to talk over with a Christian, and because she trusted him, she went out with him. She was shocked at the way he treated her. The young woman said his aggressive sexual behavior made her date with him the worst she had ever experienced. He tried to manipulate her with guilt feelings, and when that did not work he stepped up the aggression to physical force that stopped just short of rape.

My heart broke for this young woman when I heard her story. I thanked God that her authentic experience of the love of Christ was powerful enough to keep her going through the confusing and painful period following that horrible evening spent with a sinfully driven and obsessed young man who claimed to be a Christian.

This kind of sexual aggressiveness by single men on dates is common today. And it is no longer thought to be the result of an abnormal psychological disposition. Mary Koralewski, a researcher at Purdue University, says that most incarcerated rapists can be shown to have deficiencies that lead to their aggressive behavior, but such deficiencies are not present in college men who would be likely to perpetrate "date rape." She and a colleague surveyed 300 Purdue men enrolled in introductory psychology classes and found that ten per cent had engaged in forced sexual intercourse and fifty per cent had been involved in some kind of coercive sexual behavior, from forced kissing to oral sex. Their conclusion in the study was that this kind of common aggressive behavior is simply the result of the "callous sexual attitudes" of our time.[7]

The church continues to drift in this area as it is invaded with the permissive and destructive attitudes of the world toward sex. I was surprised and upset to read in an official singles publication for my denomination an incredibly irresponsible article entitled (ironically) "Responsible Sex and the Christian Single." Author David Ratcliff, associate pastor of Collegiate Presbyterian Church in Ames, Iowa, writes: "Many single persons will choose celibacy as their lifestyle before marriage. I affirm this as one option. . . . There are other singles who will express their sexuality in committed relationships outside of marriage. I affirm this as well if it is expressed within the context of mutual love and not as shallow 'one night stands.' "[8]

Stop for a moment and think this through. This argument for the right to have genital sex based on feelings of love makes sex a possible chosen option for any two people who begin to have such feelings. Young teens can have these feelings for each other. Married adults can feel love for someone other than their marriage partners. If we argue for the freedom to have genital sex with anyone for whom we have feelings of love, the long-term potential for pain and harm is immense. This is an incredibly immature position for anyone to take today. Even smart secular publications are recognizing the dangers of live-in relationships.[9]

There may be no power as destructive, when it is abused, as sexual power. But on the other hand, there may be no power as constructive when it is managed. Sex can be a power to build for the kingdom when single men and women today choose to manage its power. I have known many men and women who became Christians because the Christian man or woman they were dating would not manipulate them sexually, trying to use their date to gain something for themselves. It is wonderfully refreshing for a woman today to date a man who is interested in her as a person, a man who would never do anything that had the potential to diminish her.

Paul's advice is good in this area. In a scriptural context dealing with sexual immorality he says, "Let no one deceive you with empty words . . ." (Eph 5:6). We need to be clear on the biblical teaching regarding our sexuality. And when our behavior and attitudes toward sex are grounded in the wise parameters of God, there is potential for joy, freedom and blessing in all of our relationships with others.

It has to be emphasized here that genital sex is only one part of our complete gift of sexuality. Beautiful and fulfilling relationships between men and between men and women are possible, should be sought after, and should be celebrated as expressions of God's gift of sexuality for the single man. Intimacy does not demand participation in the full physical dimension of sexuality.

Single men can enjoy relationships that are wholesome and alive with authentic love and caring. Affectionate relationships without genital sex are completely possible and deeply rewarding. There is a joy-filled blessing of relationship available for the single man who wants to live appropriately under God as a member of Christ's body.

Only a mature single man will experience this intimacy. It takes maturity in Christ to manage the strong physical and emotional sexual responses that usually occur first when a man meets a woman attractive to him. Our physical desires are not wrong; they are normal and healthy. However, they have to be controlled or we never get beyond them to enjoy the other rewarding dimensions of relating freely as a whole person to the opposite sex.

Paul says, "We take captive every thought to make it obedient to Christ" (2 Cor 10:5). In another letter he guides Timothy by saying, "Flee the evil desires of youth, and pursue righteousness, faith, love and peace, along with those who call on the Lord out of a pure heart" (2 Tim 2:22). It is not easy to give verses like these a pre-eminent place in your life. It is especially tough to consistently apply them in an area like sexuality where temptations are powerfully charged. But the wonderful, ongoing reward of enjoying love and peace in your relationships with women instead of the constant inner tension caused by unbridled lust will convince you that God's way is truly the better way.

God will bless your righteous desire to fill your mind with what is pleasing to him. He will help you to grow from selfishness to selflessness in the sexual area. Your reward will be intimate relationships of love, trust and mutual respect that you may not have dreamed possible.

Gaining Control

If we are serious about making headway against the powers of sexual addiction, there are some things to think about that might bring help.

First, refuse to rationalize the problem. Name it. Admit the addiction. Admit your powerlessness to gain control over the obsession. You will make no progress if you cannot accept the fact that you have a real problem in the area of sexual control.

Also important is to risk bringing the problem out in the open. Talk to a pastor or friend or Christian counselor. If you are in a men's group, work to develop the group intimacy to the place where you can support each other in dealing with sexual temptations. Sexual problems are particularly difficult to manage as

long as they are our private secret. We often keep these things
secret because we like the experiences we are having more than
we really want to be freed of the obsession. It takes great
strength to want God's will enough to confess your sin to another and form an accountable relationship. But God will bless
this kind of sincere attempt at spiritual growth and progress.

Take advantage of God's call to repentance. When you are
deeply moved about the nature of your sin, open your heart
and life to God. Confess your sin and listen for his guidance.
Repentance is always the first step toward authentic renewal.

Think about the price you are paying for your addiction.
Consider the effect of your practice on the relationships of
those you love. What effect might this sin have on your wife,
your children, your work, your progress in school? What if this
practice picks up intensity and builds to another level, then
another? What is the cost at that level? Are you willing to pay
it? Think of the emotional pain the sin is exacting on you. At
the same time, think of the peace and freedom that could be
yours if you would step with God into the future of a new life
and never look back. You pay an enormous price for sexual sin
in guilt, shame and low self-esteem.

Remind yourself of the biblical meanings for our human
sexuality. The more we appreciate the beauty and wonder of
God's gracious gift of sexuality, the less we will be able to demean the gift. If we really love God and love those he has
created, sexual sin will become increasingly impossible for us.
Our love of God will carry us out of bondage.

Consider what you are actually doing when you enter into
sexual sin. A friend of mine told me that once he realized that
the young women he gazed at in magazines were daughters of
men like himself, about the same age as his own daughter, he
could not look with pleasure into the magazines again. A flash
of daylight from an outside door of a theater destroys the illusion of reality on the screen. A dose of reality thinking can do

the same for our illogical fantasies.

Make a record of the steps in your normal process that lead you toward a sexual sin. Learn to stop the process at the earliest possible stage to gain control before the sexual drive gains strength and is too powerful to stop. Don't go near the magazine racks. Don't arrange a meeting with that particular woman. Erase the videotapes and get rid of the magazines. Control your environment to make it holy rather than an environment filled with temptation, alive with possibility for sexual sin.

Trace as well as you can the history of your obsession. Sometimes we need professional help to do this, but all behavior springs from need. Learning the need-basis for your sexual behavior can be a great help in understanding how to overcome it. You can work toward achieving satisfaction of your needs in appropriate and healthy ways once you understand what they really are. Some sexual problems are related to the way your parents viewed or practiced sex, or they are rooted in your relationship with your mother or your father. Our insecurities drive our sexual behaviors. Without the courage to relate, we will often settle for far less than God would want for us.

If you are married, turn your sexual energies toward your wife. Even your fantasies can be directed toward your marriage partner rather than toward other women. This is an effort on our part to leave the old ways behind and move on with God to a new level. Paul writes: "In a large house there are articles not only of gold and silver, but also of wood and clay; some are for noble purposes and some for ignoble. If a man cleanses himself from the latter, he will be an instrument for noble purposes, made holy, useful to the Master and prepared to do any good work" (2 Tim 2:20-21).

A Husband and His Wife

Pray for your marriage relationship. Ask God to continue to build your love for your wife. As you give yourself to her in love and pray that God will bless your relationship, you may be amazed at how quickly your taste for true relationship grows. God wants your life to be filled with receiving and giving love. This is the ultimate human experience. Don't settle for less.

The more we concentrate on our marriage exclusively, the stronger the relationship becomes. If a man will take seriously his posture toward marriage recommended by Paul, "Husbands, love your wives, just as Christ loved the church and gave himself up for her" (Eph 5:25), a rich and blessed lifelong marriage relationship is always a possibility. How did Christ love the church? When we were the least lovable, scarred with life and deeply sinful, he loved us so much that he would give his life to make us whole. The verse challenges us to learn to love sacrificially. Our single aim in this area should be to give ourselves fully to our marriages, consistently acting in love toward our wives, caring about their happiness and loving them as they are, lifting them at every opportunity to the highest level of appreciation in our thoughts and as we speak about them to others.

If we will choose to love our wives selflessly even as we live in this real world of imperfect bodies, imperfect personalities, imperfect sexual experiences, we will enter into and enjoy— beyond what we might have ever imagined—that which God blessed, mysterious unity biblically described as "one flesh" under God in Christ. A fantasy world will never deliver this kind of real and lasting blessing.

Growing in love over a lifetime takes intentionality. It takes a dedicated refusal to be duped by the sexual lies. It takes consistent prayer and a willing desire to be a one-woman man.

May your fountain be blessed,
> and may you rejoice in the wife of your youth.

A loving doe, a graceful deer—
> may her breasts satisfy you always, may you ever be
> captivated by her love.

Proverbs 5:18, 19

Questions for Groups and Individuals

1. What are some of God's purposes behind creating us male and female? (p. 57)

2. What evidence do you see that our society has lost sight of God's purposes for sex?

3. What pressures from society (for instance, the media), make it difficult for you to resist sexual temptations?

4. Are there ways you could "clean up your environment" and remove some of the stimuli that tempt you to sexual sin?

5. Various strategies for gaining control over sexual sin are suggested in this chapter. (pp. 73-75) Are any of these ideas new to you?

Which do you think may be the most helpful for you?

6. Share with others insights or strategies you have discovered that have helped you in your struggle against sexual temptation.

4/THE TEMPTATION TO HAVE AN AFFAIR

Hell is the only place outside of heaven
where we can be safe from the dangers of love.

C. S. LEWIS

*T*here is no story more telling of the tragic consequences of an adulterous affair than the biblical story of David and Bathsheba.

King David was the greatest king of biblical history, a faithful man whose heart belonged to God. One evening, from the roof of his palace, he watched a beautiful woman bathe. He inquired about her and found out she was Bathsheba, wife of Uriah the Hittite, one of David's soldiers who was away on battle duty. David sent for Bathsheba and slept with her. She became pregnant.

David decided to try to cover up the sin. He called Uriah home from the field, expecting that the soldier would sleep with his wife while on furlough. The noble Uriah would not go home and sleep in pleasure while his fellow soldiers were sleeping in tents and engaged in battle. Uriah slept on the palace steps two evenings in a row. Frustrated, David sent him back to the front carrying sealed orders to place Uriah at the head of the battle where the fighting was fiercest. Uriah was killed in battle. Out of fear that his sin would become known, King David had murdered a loyal soldier who would have gladly and freely given his life for the king he loved (2 Sam 11).

The statistics on the frequency of affairs today are disheartening. After reviewing the recent literature, Reiss and Thompson indicate that forty to fifty per cent of all married men have extramarital affairs. Nearly seventy per cent of all married men under forty expect to have an extramarital relationship. Given the increasingly permissive views toward sex today, researchers Gilbert Nass and Roger Libby have predicted that between one-half and two-thirds of all husbands will have an affair before they reach age forty.[1]

Perhaps even more disturbing (although not surprising) for us as Christians is the result of a poll conducted recently by the research department of *Christianity Today*. They asked pastors in the U.S., "Have you ever had sexual intercourse with someone other than your spouse since you've been in local-church ministry?" Of the respondents, twelve per cent answered yes. Of the eighty-eight per cent who answered no, many chose to write along with the answer that their sexual purity had not come easily. Pastors were also asked, "Have you ever had other forms of sexual contact with someone other than your spouse, i.e. passionate kissing, fondling/mutual masturbation, since you've been in local church ministry?" Eighteen per cent answered yes.

Christianity Today further tested its results by polling a larger Christian population with the same questions. From a random sample of a thousand subscribers to the magazine, forty-five per cent marked that they had acted inappropriately, and twenty-three per cent had experienced extramarital intercourse. These responses nearly doubled the percentages in the poll for professional ministers.[2] If the statistics are this high among readers of *Christianity Today*, then how much higher must they be in the general Christian population? They may approximate the population at large.

Few extramarital affairs end in murder, although some do. The story of David and Bathsheba is certainly unusual in this sense. But all extramarital affairs produce extraordinary pain for those who are involved in the affair and those who are innocent but relationally connected.

This powerful and honest account of a broken marriage seen through the eyes of a young girl appeared in the Girl Scout magazine, *American Girl*. It was titled, "That's the Way Life Goes Sometimes."

When I was ten, my parents got a divorce. Naturally, my father told me about it, because he was my favorite.

"Honey, I know it's been kind of bad for you these past few days, and I don't want to make it worse. But there's something I have to tell you. Honey, your mother and I got a divorce."

"But, Daddy—"

"I know you don't want this, but it has to be done. Your mother and I just don't get along like we used to. I'm already packed and my plane is leaving in half an hour."

"But, Daddy, why do you have to leave?"

"Well, honey, your mother and I can't live together anymore."

"I know that, but I mean why do you have to leave town?"

"Oh. Well, I got someone waiting for me in New Jersey."

"But, Daddy, will I ever see you again?"

"Sure you will, honey. We'll work something out."

"But what? I mean, you'll be living in New Jersey, and I'll be living here in Washington."

"Maybe your mother will agree to you spending two weeks in the summer and two in the winter with me."

"Why not more often?"

"I don't think she'll agree to two weeks in the summer and two in the winter, much less more."

"Well, it can't hurt to try."

"I know, honey, but we'll have to work it out later. My plane leaves in twenty minutes and I've got to get to the airport. Now I'm going to get my luggage, and I want you to go to your room so you don't have to watch me. And no long goodbyes either."

"Okay, Daddy. Goodbye. Don't forget to write."

"I won't. Goodbye. Now go to your room."

"Okay. Daddy, I don't want you to go!"

"I know, honey. But I have to."

"Why?"

"You wouldn't understand, honey."

"Yes, I would."

"No, you wouldn't."

"Oh well. Goodbye."

"Goodbye. Now go to your room. Hurry up."

"Okay. Well, I guess that's the way life goes sometimes."

"Yes honey. That's the way life goes sometimes."

After my father walked out that door, I never heard from him again.[3]

This piece in my file has helped me to hold in my mind and heart the reality of the pain caused by the selfishness and sin of an affair.

The sin of adultery is condemned throughout Scripture. Leviticus 18:20 reads, "Do not have intercourse with your neighbor's wife and defile yourself with her." The sin was regarded as so harmful that its punishment was death (Lev 20:10). The New Testament also warns against adultery. Hebrews 13:4 says, "Marriage should be honored by all, and the marriage bed kept

pure, for God will judge the adulterer and all the sexually immoral" (see also 1 Cor 6:9; Jas 4:4).

What is adultery? It is explicitly a voluntary sexual encounter
of a married person with anyone other than his lawfully
wedded spouse. Sometimes adultery occurs as an extramarital
encounter, or one-night stand. This kind of encounter lacks the
ongoing attraction and intense involvement that characterize
the extramarital affair that has progressed in relationship over
time. The one-night stand, however, still has enormous potential for harm in a relationship. For one thing, it can grow into
a full-fledged affair. But even if a relationship does not develop,
the sin will deeply affect the persons who have had the encounter.

All sexual sin is powerful and memorable. A Christian cannot
indulge in sexual sin lightly. We cannot play with sex like we
play tennis. Anyone who thinks he can be a sexual dilettante
is in for a painful surprise. Life changes when adultery occurs.
There is always the cover-up. There are lies, pretenses, suspicion, and if the truth surfaces, trust in the marriage relationship
is often irreparably damaged. There will be relational consequences. King David's sin was apparently a one-night encounter. That one-night stand led to murder.

The long-term affair which includes cohabitation is even
more devastating to everyone involved. The man and woman
in this situation develop an intense emotional preoccupation
and share repeated acts of sexual intercourse. The affair becomes an obsession. Everything from career success to the
health of family life is deeply threatened by this adulterous
relationship. For the Christian, the affair destroys credibility
and witness. Think for a moment of the nationally known
Christian leaders who have suffered as a result of this kind of
indiscretion. The emotional and psychological trauma of the
affair in the life of the Christian is devastating. David's deeply
real description of the aftermath of sin in the believer's life is

worth reading in this context:

> O Lord, do not rebuke me in your anger
>   or discipline me in your wrath.
> For your arrows have pierced me,
>   and your hand has come down upon me.
> Because of your wrath there is no health in my body;
>   my bones have no soundness because of my sin.
> My guilt has overwhelmed me
>   like a burden too heavy to bear.
> My wounds fester and are loathsome
>   because of my sinful folly.
> I am bowed down and brought very low;
>   all day long I go about mourning.
> My back is filled with searing pain;
>   there is no health in my body.
> I am feeble and utterly crushed;
>   I groan in anguish of heart. (Ps 38:1-8)

Knowing the pain that will inevitably result from living in sin should make us want to do everything we can to keep from being caught in the ugly snare of adultery.

There is another kind of affair that is also damaging. I know a man who lives with his wife out of duty to the marriage bond, but gives his affection to another woman. He does not have a physical sexual relationship with the other woman. In this he feels he meets the biblical requirement of marriage fidelity and is not guilty of committing adultery. Yet the marriage is defiled by this kind of behavior.

In a very real way this man turns his wife into his whore. He gives all of his affection to the other woman and uses his wife to meet his physical sexual need. Our wives—and no one else—should be the focus of our loving affection for the opposite sex. This situation reminds me of so many of the sins of the Pharisees. They kept the law in their external behavior, but were often far from its loving intent. Jesus was quick to condemn such legalistic claims of self-righteousness.

How Affairs Happen

Extramarital affairs most often occur without conscious premeditation. If we tried people today for having affairs, few would be found guilty of adultery in the first degree. Men and women usually slip into a relationship with someone and soon find that they are deeply involved and it is difficult to disentangle themselves.

Two factors combine to create a situation ripe for the affair. There has to be an emotional readiness and a timely opportunity. We often hear in counseling, "I was an affair waiting to happen."

Modern movies, books, TV soaps and sitcoms all promote the notion that extramarital sex is a diversion that can add interest and entertainment to our present dull existence. If any risk or harm is hinted at in the media, it is usually tenuously presented in contrast to the strong promise of increased pleasure, excitement, warmth and caring for the person courageous enough to risk the new relationship. This media blitz, coupled with the contemporary demise of American morality, creates an environment ripe for sexual promiscuity. This immoral stance of our society toward promiscuity is a major influence which emotionally and psychologically prepares men and women to be open to the possibility of an extramarital affair.

The condition of a marriage also contributes to a person's readiness for an affair. If there is tension in the marriage relationship, it is easy to see an outside person as the answer to all life's problems. Couples with unresolved relational difficulties, money problems, or unhealthy or unrewarding sexual lives within the marriage can become candidates for an outside relationship. Whenever the home begins to represent tension in the minds of married couples and outside friendships with the opposite sex promise relationship without the hassle, there is potential danger.

One situation that happens with young couples is such a common contributor to the affair that it deserves special mention here. In young families where children come into the picture quickly, the demands of motherhood can keep Mom in the home with two or three little ones. Her work is essential and good, but the tasks of motherhood are usually full-time. There is little opportunity at this stage for continued personal and intellectual growth. At the same time her young husband is just beginning to take off in his career. He trains and travels and meets interesting people every day. His job often takes him out of the home, away from his wife and family.

Their growth paths diverge. Suddenly the husband feels he has nothing in common with the wife of his youth. They have not attended to the need to continue to grow together as a couple. The husband may find someone in the office who shares more of his interests. The wife may find someone in the neighborhood or at church who accepts and appreciates her as she is and extends love and caring. Young couples need to find ways to continue growing in their relationship together. Otherwise they become prime candidates for the extramarital relationship.

The other life stage that has great potential for going wrong is the time of a man's mid-life transition. This is such an important topic in relation to marriage fidelity that I have chosen to take it up in more depth later in this chapter.

The main point is that any unresolved marital tension can contribute to a person's readiness for an extramarital affair. This is why it is so important for husbands and wives to work very hard at their marriages and to get help with any problems that persist in their relationship.

There are also many personal factors that contribute to a readiness to have an affair. The influence of our upbringing can be an important factor. Poor parental models and lack of love in our parent's marriage can create a psychological disposition toward brokenness in our marriage. Or a lenient up-bringing can set up patterns of self-indulgence. An overly strict upbringing can promote feelings of being trapped in a marriage, or struggles with authority in relationship. Lack of maturity of individuals, or emotional instability, or poor self-image, or depression, or any number of other emotional, physical or psychological problems can create a readiness for an affair, either in the person with the problem or in the person's mate.

The quality of our relationships with Christ is also of paramount importance. Are we strong in Christ, or have we let our faith go and let the world inch its way into our lives? Again, it is extremely important to get help with any personal difficulties that might contribute to problems in our marriages. We should feel no shame for seeking professional help to keep our marriages strong. The only really shameful thing is to stand by and do nothing, letting our marriage fall apart before it even has a chance to grow into the beautiful relationship it was meant to be.

These societal factors, marital pressures and personal and spiritual realities by themselves or in combination can create the emotional readiness for an extramarital relationship. Once the readiness quotient is present, all that is needed for a man to respond favorably is the right woman in the wrong place and at the wrong time. If we want to stand for God in our marriages, we should fight this battle on two fronts. We will first work to eliminate any problems that could potentially lead to either our own or our spouse's readiness to become involved with another person. Second, we need to study and understand how affairs happen to fine couples with good marriages.

My psychologist friend Jay tells me that nearly half of the men who come to him trying to sort out how they got involved with another woman (and how they can end the relationship and rebuild their marriages) have good marriages. They are men you would never believe would slip into an affair: bright, happy men who love their wives and families.

What did they miss? How did it happen?

The Affair Analyzed

There are twelve common steps[4] that usually occur in sequence as a relationship moves toward an adulterous affair. These steps often occur over a long period of time, but a man and a woman can move through these stages of relationship in a single evening. Becoming aware of the steps helps us to recognize what might be happening to us so we can stop the process before we are in over our heads.

Our two enemies here are rationalization and denial. We rationalize when we give acceptable reasons for unacceptable thoughts, feelings and behaviors. Denial is our often intense refusal to recognize the truth about our thoughts, feelings and behaviors. The writer of Hebrews was aware of how sin can harden our hearts and darken our understanding, turning us away from God. He writes, "But encourage one another daily, as long as it is called Today, so that none of you may be hardened by sin's deceitfulness" (Heb 3:13).

Jay has shared with me how far from reason the rationalization can get. One woman he was seeing in his practice said, "Isn't it wonderful that God has given me two handsome men to love." Another woman thought that God understood and accepted her numerous affairs because, after all, it was he who created within her this need for other men. A man in counseling said, "It's okay, because each time we have sex we end by praying together."

Rationalization working hand-in-hand with denial can alter our sense of reality and make us less and less able and willing to recognize that we are moving toward a fall. It is amazing the extent to which we can explain and justify our sinful behavior. Rationalization and denial play a part at each step in the process of entanglement.

1. *Readiness.* The first step is the condition of emotional readiness already discussed in some detail above. Something is occurring in a man's life that has him leaning away from the marriage.

If we look closely at the story of David and Bathsheba in 2 Samuel 11, it appears that this kind of emotional readiness was present in David. Several things indicate that his situation was abnormal. It was spring, "the time that kings go off to war," but David did not go. He stayed at home (v. 1). David was in bed, but could not sleep. He got out of bed to walk around the roof of the palace (v. 2). Why was he having trouble sleeping? Why had he not accompanied his troops into battle?

David is thought to be about thirty-nine years old at this time. He has been a great soldier and has won countless battles. Now he stays in Jerusalem and sends his troops out. Has the king not kept himself in prime physical shape? Is he the picture of the fading football hero? Does he suffer from self-doubt? Is he entering what we know today as mid-life crisis? Whatever is happening to David at this moment in his life, he seems vulnerable, emotionally ready for the affair. David sees Bathsheba bathing. He wastes no time finding out who she is. Her husband is away. He sends for her without delay (v. 3-4).

We can learn from David's fall. When we sense a slight leaning away from our relationship with the woman we love, we can take action to protect ourselves during this time of vulnerability. We can work to understand what is happening to us and turn our energy toward regaining the full health of our relationship.

2. *Alertness.* The second stage in the affair process is a growing awareness of a particular person in our web of relationships. We may begin simply by thinking occasionally about the other person. The innocent thoughts can turn to fantasizing about her. As she becomes more present in our conscious thoughts, she may begin to appear in dreams as well. The dreams are often filled with sexual fantasy.

Sometimes a man in this stage will shoot group photographs where the woman is present at an office party or at a get-together of families on a holiday. The man then finds himself returning to the snapshots again and again. It is not unusual for the man in this stage to try to mentally capture the woman who is becoming a strong focus of interest. Masturbating while fantasizing about the woman is common.

The rationalization developed is that there is no harm in fantasizing. It's only human.

3. *Innocent Meeting*. During the time of heightened awareness of the other woman, there can be truly innocent, chance meetings, often legitimate business contacts that can potentially build the relationship. This is the stage where some flirtation can develop, prolonged eye contact, interchange of harmless-sounding sexual innuendo, enticing body language. Both people involved at this point would deny any real interest in each other.

4. *Intentional Meeting*. Meetings occur frequently which appear to be by chance when in reality one person has acted in such a way as to increase the likelihood of meeting. This stage is often humorously portrayed in films. A man is shown waiting for hours at a particular street corner. When the woman appears, he walks up to her and acts surprised as if she's the last person in the world he thought he'd see. In real life this stage could be humorous too if it weren't so sad. This kind of game-playing has an adolescent flavor to it. It proves that the excitement of attraction to the opposite sex can overpower our rational side. Sexual attraction can easily make fools out of us. At this point a person enters a real danger zone.

5. *Public Lingering*. The man and woman now spend time together while in group settings. They will tend to shut others out by turning away from the group and avoiding eye contact with others. There is a growing interest in each other at this point. Topics of conversation include personal history, interests

in sports, politics, business. Observers might pick up something unusual about the relationship at this stage. I've had the experience of trying to break into a conversation between a man and woman in this stage and being treated as an unwanted intruder. But the man and woman would still deny any suggestion that this was more than normal adult relating. The public setting helps the couple to rationalize. The man thinks: "It's fine to focus on her. Nothing can happen. We're with others."

6. *Private Lingering*. Soon the man and woman find that they are still together long after the others have left. There is now a growing excitement in being together alone. It is a seductive feeling, enticing. Conversation shifts from ideas to feelings. Caring is shared. There is an entry through conversation into private and personal areas. The man and woman still feel fine about the relationship because the meetings begin in public.

7. *Purposeful Isolating*. Now the man and woman begin to plan times alone for "legitimate" purposes. The man asks the woman if she will meet and help him sort out his marital problems. Or the woman asks the man to stay late at the office to lend his expertise to a certain project she's trying to wrap up. The couple would still deny any suggestion that their relationship was not completely appropriate. At home the man's wife might notice a decrease in verbal and nonverbal communication. He seems suddenly detached, cool, almost formal in his relating. There may be uncompleted phone calls.

I stayed with a couple recently while doing some work at their church. The husband came home exhausted from work on Friday. He went right to bed and slept for an hour and a half. When he got up he grabbed a quick bite of supper and returned to work. He worked on Saturday afternoon and also had to work on Sunday. When he was at home I felt that he was deeply troubled. He was aloof and uninvolved in the conversations going on around him. His wife was worried about him working so much at night and about the tremendous stress he seemed to be carrying. She talked with him constantly about finding another job that would not be so demanding on his time. She worried about his health. I was not surprised to learn from her a few months later that he had been involved in a secret affair and had moved out of the house.

8. *Pleasurable Isolating.* Now the man and woman are planning times alone with each other for the sheer enjoyment and fun of being together. The relationship takes on a youthful euphoria. There is the shared experience of excitement and adventure. There is more intimacy. The man and woman are touching. There is a warm touch to the hand or arm, or the hand is slipped around the waist. During this stage, the spouse will often notice that there are large blocks of time not accounted for. There is a noticeable decrease in pleasurable times together in the marriage. The man and woman will still rationalize the relationship by saying that adults need good friends of the opposite sex. There is nothing wrong with being good friends.

9. *Affectionate Embracing.* Secret longings for each other become intense. There is embracing without letting go. There is increased touching and playful caressing. Childish games like tickling and wrestling are often played at this stage to increase the physical contact. The rationalization is that there is nothing wrong with physically expressing support for one another. At the same time with their spouses, there will be a decrease in affectionate embracing and physical contact.

10. *Passionate Embracing.* Affectionate touching and embracing lead to passionate interchanges. When alcohol is involved, a couple moves quickly through these stages. Anything that reduces inhibitions contributes to the increased physical desire and expression. The couple will still rationalize and say that it is fine to get aroused because it is innocent and unplanned. "Besides, my wife no longer makes me feel this way," the man thinks.

11. *Capitulation.* The couple gives in to sexual intercourse. Denial is eliminated at this stage. There is no way that they can deny the reality of what has occurred between them.

12. *Acceptance.* Here the man and woman admit to themselves and to each other that they are truly having an affair. If they continue their relationship from this point, it is out of mutual choice. Here the emotional investment in the affair is at its peak, and the emotional investment in the marriage is at its lowest point. The spouse is almost always aware by this time. Her husband is home less. He is frequently away overnight without explanation. He may even find a creative way to allow his wife to discover the affair. The tension of living a double life is usually too much for someone to bear for very long.

Is this the end of the story? Do the man and woman live happily ever after? No. The story of an affair is not a comedy. It is a tragedy.

Welcome to the Real World

Jim Dobson has said, "The grass is greener on the other side of the fence, but it still has to be mowed." Once the excitement of the early stages of the affair wears off, the new couple is forced to live real life again, life in the common place. The man and woman suddenly have to face and work through personality adjustments. They discover spiritual, emotional and physical imperfections in each other that they had never noticed before. Someone has to fix the cars, cook the meals, clean the house, run errands, struggle with the finances.

There is now a trail of pain like a cancer that eats away at the new relationship. Kids have been hurt. A wife and a husband have been abandoned. The complex and difficult relational network is hard to manage. And, in the new relationship there is always the underlying suspicion, especially as marital tensions begin to grow again, that the new partner will opt out—try his or her luck again with another. "After all, he did it with me," the new wife may think. Second marriages are nearly twice as likely as first marriages to end in divorce.[5]

My parents took me to a small local circus when I was a young child. It was an exciting, memorable experience for me. I was thrilled by the men and women on the flying trapeze, the high wire act, the clowns, the wild animals, the glitter of the costumes and the bright colored lights. We ate snowcones. I had never had one before. The smell of popcorn and the sound of the ringmaster's voice live in my memory.

Not too many years ago Judie and I took our small children to a local circus in Minnesota. The experience was very different for me as an adult. I watched my kids. They were absolutely taken by the same glitter and excitement that had captivated me when I was their age. This time I watched them react and compared what they were seeing to what I saw.

They were completely unaware of the seedy side of the cheap circus that made a negative impression on me. They missed the large, gaping holes in the nylons of the women performers. They didn't see the emptiness on the faces of the circus men and women who looked to me a little desperate, as if imprisoned by a bad set of circumstances in this third-rate organization. My children overlooked the broken-down, patched-up equipment, the smell of dung on filthy animals, the fact that the snowcones were all ice with only a trickle of watery coloring poured over them. They loved it. I was glad for them.

Like wide-eyed children we enter into extramarital affairs. Our eyes are open, but for some reason we are blind to many of the realities that will become devastatingly apparent later when the glitter wears off. It is all right to be childlike in some of the areas of our lives. But we have to live in the real world. Yes, we want desperately for the new relationship to work, to give us the pleasure, the romance, the affirmation we felt was lacking in our former marriage. But we have bought the lie, the hype, the barker's voice and the colored lights—the propaganda that says we can have everything we want simply by changing partners in mid-stream. It is very American to seek the quick fix; we are looking for the easy road to the real thing.

It is truly a tragedy. Men and women change partners again and again chasing the illusion. Many die lonely, empty people, lacking love.

Is the cup of your marriage half-empty? Or half-full? The thing to do is to recognize the time spent in your present relationship as an investment to be nurtured. Your marriage is like a good retirement plan. As long as you keep the deposits flowing, the account grows. The marriage develops like compound interest over time. Small investments of love and nurture reap great dividends in relational happiness. No one in their right mind would squander a solid investment account that has been growing through the years to take up a shaky, speculative venture. It does not make good sense. If the grass is greener on the other side of the fence, you should try watering your own.

There is no easy road to authentic relationship. It takes hard work. If you feel the pleasure has gone out of your marriage, or the romance, or that the marriage is not meeting your basic need for encouragement and love, then you have work to do. I'm sorry, but there is no other way. The only action that makes sense is to dig in and recommit yourself to your present marriage. Why has the pleasure left? Do you need to have more time away together as a couple? Are you taking advantage of every opportunity to have fun together and rekindle some of the earlier flame? What is it in the relationship that is not meeting your needs? Why not talk with your wife about this? It is difficult for you as a man to admit that you have needs, especially emotional needs. But my experience tells me that wives are usually good at listening if their husbands will only begin talking. Honest dialog will build great strength into your marriage. Again, you may need help from a skilled third person to get this kind of real sharing started.

A good marriage is worth any amount of work you may need to invest in it. No other endeavor pays such rich dividends over time. Please, don't be duped. Resist the lie that another woman might be the answer to all your problems. There is no benefit in starting over from scratch. You will only live from brokenness to brokenness without success. Learn how to fill your half-full cup to the brim.

The Good Fight
There are numerous things we can do to fight the temptation to stray from our marriages and families.

1. *Build the Marriage Relationship.* Having a good marriage will reduce the readiness of the marriage partners for an affair.

Communication is the key here. Staying in touch with each other's feelings, pressures and tensions will keep you focused on where your relationship needs work. Caring enough to meet these mutual needs in your marriage will help make your relationship a meaningful one in which to be involved. This kind of communication requires time. Make time for each other.

Judie and I went on a weekend together in Colorado shortly after moving to Boulder. We had four small children at the time. It seemed almost more work than it was worth arranging care for the kids all weekend. Once on the road we realized that we had not been away from the kids alone together since Jana was a baby. It had been six years.

The weekend did not turn out to be one of our best experiences, but in a way it was one of the most helpful to our relationship. Often during the three days and two nights, we sat and stared at each other with nothing to say. We had let our relationship get away from us. The kids had been the center of everything for too long. It was good to recognize the problem early. What if we had continued our pattern of lack of communication until the kids were gone? There would be nothing left of our marriage. Judie and I talked about it all weekend. We dedicated ourselves to finding regular time together without the kids so that we could continue to grow closer in our relationship over the years.

Do fun and interesting things together as a couple. Talk regularly with each other about the important things in your life. Take advantage of opportunities to learn and grow together as a couple whenever possible. Take classes together on marriage topics. Go to marriage encounters. Read and study books together on marriage and family topics. Be intentional in building your marriage in this way. If you have to be on separate paths for a while, talk constantly about your individual experiences. Let your spouse share in your work life and be sure you share in hers. Another important way to develop intimacy is to practice spiritual disciplines as a couple. Study the Bible together, even if you just read one verse a day, discuss it briefly and spend a few minutes in prayer. God will bless your earnest attempts to draw near to him and to have a Christ-centered marriage.

Fill your mind with thoughts about your wife and kids. Keep reminders of your family with you, pictures of your wife and kids at the office, in your wallet. When I am traveling, the first thing I do in a strange motel room is take the family pictures out and put them on the dresser or mirror where I can see them and think about them and pray for them while I'm gone. Keep regular contact with your family by phone if you have to travel.

Talk over with your wife what you would consider appropriate relating with the opposite sex. Decide together what is acceptable for the two of you. Is it proper for you to have lunch with a female associate? Once? Twice? How many times? How often? Work on reasonable limits toward relating to others with which both of you feel comfortable. This will guard your marriage. If an unusual circumstance occurs that would be outside of your agreed-upon behavior, share it. Don't hide it, or dismiss it as unimportant. There will be times when exceptions from your rules are necessary.

Work together on the romance factors in your marriage. Get creative in gift giving and sharing notes of love and appreciation. It's not that these things become less meaningful after we have been married for a while, it is that we stop thinking creatively and arranging the little surprises that were common for us when we were dating. Surprise parties and expressions of caring that cost something for you to plan are ways to say, "I love you" and keep the romance in your lives.

2. *The Affair Process.* Think through again the twelve-step affair process. Measure your behavior against the steps. Are you at step one right now? Or step two? Do you find yourself fantasizing about someone in your work circle? Or a neighbor? Or a friend's wife? Don't be caught off guard. Don't let rationalization and denial build your readiness for relationship with a woman outside your marriage. Keeping a clear head about the stages will help you to avoid the common traps. For instance, if you recognize that you are lingering in public, start avoiding contact. This will sometimes be a real battle. But I guarantee you it is easier to stop the behavior at level five than at level eleven. Be tough with yourself. Be accountable to your wife and to friends for your behavior. Accept insights and the awareness of friends and your spouse when they suggest that you may be playing with fire in a relationship.

The most important idea to remember is that all sin starts in the mind. If we control it there, it cannot grow. Turn your sexual fantasies toward your marriage. Control your thoughts. Even pray for good dreams. God will help you manage this sexual dimension of your life.

3. *Walk with God.* Foundational to gaining strength to resist temptation is a life lived in God. I can remember times in my life when I felt spiritually flat and emotionally exhausted. I know how vulnerable I was. I thank God daily for the many

times he has protected me when I have not had the good sense to take care of myself.

Be regular in fellowship with Christians. Be regular in worship. Be regular in your devotional life. I have found my men's Bible study to be an essential part of the spiritual foundation for my life. Men need to have a place where they can discuss openly and honestly with other men the tensions and problems they encounter in life. If you are not in a study like this, seek one. Make certain it has the element of personal sharing in it. Also, find your place of ministry through your local church. Where can you serve God with your gifts? Being in a place of service for God helps us to be accountable in our lives. For instance, we will tend to resist sin if we know that we have to get up in front of fifth-graders next Sunday and talk with them about how important it is for them to guard their lives in Christ.

If you have had a hard time getting started in the spiritual area, talk with your pastor about it. Be willing to admit that you are just beginning. Don't let your male ego stand in the way of doing what you know is right. On the other hand, if you have walked long with the Lord, guard against being complacent about God. Our relationships with Christ take continual work and energy at every level. Real moral strength and decisive action will increasingly mark our lives as we daily fall more deeply in love with God.

4. *Count the Cost.* Perhaps it will help us to keep our heads in the real world if we think about the consequences of infidelity. I can't help but play through my mind regularly the reality that I write books aimed at encouraging others toward a more effective life in Christ. How quickly my credibility and work in Christ could be destroyed. I know my vulnerabilities. The Devil knows them too. I am never surprised when confronted with an opportunity to sin. My prayers are that I will have godly wisdom to see through the temptations to the ugly consequences of sin. No one is immune. Many great leaders in

ministry have toppled and have never fully recovered from the consequences of a momentary transgression. It is never worth it.

I think about the fact that sin grieves the Lord I love. I think about hurting Judie and the kids. Their love toward me and trust in me are so evident. They thank God in their prayers for a family that sticks together, a family they can count on. I think about how long I have been trying to impact other family members for Christ. How quickly years of prayer and work can go down the drain.

I think about my obligation to my brothers and sisters in Christ to contribute to the positive image of Christianity in our community. We never sin in a vacuum. A pastor in Rochester, Minnesota, was driven by sexual lust to pose as a doctor and examine women in the hospitals there. I lived in Rochester when the discovery was made. Think of the devastating effect such exposure has on the minds of those who might be considering Christ. I pray that I will never contribute to this kind of breech of trust.

There are, of course, other practical matters like AIDS, venereal disease (I might even unwittingly infect Judie) and unwanted pregnancy. There are financial and career problems. There is the shame and guilt that affects the whole of your life and relationships. I'm sure you can add to this list. Somewhere near the top should be the realization that such an act would bring great delight to our enemy, Satan, who is in battle against God for our very souls.

It is important to remember that even though thinking of the consequences of our sinful action can help us resist the sin of adultery, we are only truly moral in a biblical sense when we refuse to sin primarily out of our love for God and for what he is trying to accomplish in the world. All lesser reasons are self-centered. If we choose not to sleep with our secretaries just because we might get caught and lose our job, we are thinking of ourselves. We are aiming at something different in the Christian life. Self-centered reasons for resisting sin will only help us temporarily. Use whatever works when you need it to keep from falling. But remember that self-centered motivations are never strong enough to bring consistency over the long haul.

Our goal in developing moral character is to get to the place where we act faithfully and consistently simply because to do otherwise would bring harm to the person and cause of the God we love. Thinking of suffering consequences may help us resist for a while, but only a real and lasting love for God will guard and buttress our fight for life.

High Noon in a Man's Life

The mid-life transition is a significant passage in men's lives. If it goes well, we can experience a kind of rebirth and enter the next stage with energy, purpose and a renewed sense of identity. If it goes poorly a man may stagnate at this time, withdrawing from life and resigning himself to what he considers the inevitable downward drift of life into aging and insignificance.

If you would have asked me six months ago if I thought I was a prime candidate to experience a problem during mid-life transition, I would without reserve have answered no. In fact, as I thought through writing this book, I knew I would need to address the issue somewhere. It concerned me that I would have to approach the section without personal experience. Then a few weeks ago I was shaving one morning when I noticed something that stopped me abruptly. I had hair growing out of my ears. I looked more closely. The hairs looked like those I have seen growing out of the ears of old men. It was ugly. It was disgusting. I went immediately to the closet and got a scissors. In no time flat I had exorcised the troublesome material and felt immediately relieved.

Silly, isn't it? Or is it? Later I had time to reflect on the incident. Such vanity. The hair was a sign of aging. And aging is something over which we have so little control. I can cut the hair out of my ears, but it will keep coming back. No amount of exercise or proper diet will keep hair from growing in your ears or growing thin on the top of your head. We all have to deal with the fact of our aging.

As we enter this time of mid-life transition, there will be many issues to face. All of us will make the transition. Not all of us will be in crisis as we go through. It is a time similar to an adolescent's transition from childhood to adulthood. Some young people make it through more easily than others. Some men will make the transition easily as well. Others will struggle to keep life in perspective.

Picture a trapeze artist standing on a platform with a firm grip on the bar. As he swings out into the emptiness of open space, he lets go of the bar. There are a few tense moments in mid-air before he successfully completes the leap, grasps the swinging bar across from him and makes it to the solid platform on the other side. The emotions one might feel while suspended there in mid-air—the uncertainty, the fear—are similar to the emotions a man experiences going through the mid-life transition. We move from a place of stability to a scrambled period of inner searching and uncertainty before we make our way to the other side. For a while it might feel like everything is up for grabs.

This is a time of evaluation. A man looks back over what has brought him to this place. It is like taking a last quick glance at the trapeze bar swinging away behind before turning forward and grasping the bar that will carry him toward the future. There are a number of major areas of re-evaluation that each have the potential for precipitating a crisis for a man during this stage.[6]

One thing that may occur in a man's life is a realization that he has not achieved his career goals. He had expectations for himself. Now it becomes clear that he will never make his mark at the level he had hoped. Or a man will reach many of his career goals but find that they do not bring lasting satisfaction. The problem is, a man easily gets who he is mixed up with what he does. If his feelings about himself are tied to high goal expectations, and he now realizes he will never successfully achieve his goals, this can precipitate a crisis for the man. If he thought that reaching goals would bring lasting happiness, but finds after many successes that he only feels empty, this too can precipitate a crisis.

Or a man may have given up his dream early out of the pressing necessity to provide for his young family. It was not possible with a wife and small children to finish school or get the training needed to do what he really wanted in life. So the dream is suppressed. But later, when he considers the fact that he is in the middle of his life and not happy, the dream comes back to haunt him. Time has now become his enemy. A man can feel sour toward his wife and family if he feels they have kept him from realizing a more exciting life.

Crisis also might come when a man begins to realize that the more challenging and interesting jobs are now being given to younger men and women. He is not asked to contribute his expertise as he once was. The people around him now expect less of him. He is subtly and not so subtly being asked to step aside. The man has to deal with the reality of these changes and how he responds to them through the remainder of his life.

Even family roles change. As children grow and leave home, a man's significance in the home diminishes. The children have gone their own way. They have their own homes and families. He is no longer the center of his family's life. He is not needed in the same way. A man may at this time also question the quality of his parenting. If things have not gone well with the children, he wonders if he should have spent more time with them, or disciplined them more, or loved them more.

The search for adventure at this time is also a common response to the tensions of mid-life. The man who feels mired in responsibility begins to see all aspects of the status quo as a rut. He may try radical changes. I have seen this kind of irrational action. Wives often think their husbands have gone crazy. Dad suddenly wants to sell the house and quit his job and move up in the mountains to live off the land.

A man may also come unglued when he looks in the mirror one day as I did and sees the undeniably real effect that years of gravity have had on his physical body. He joins a health club and gets into an intense exercise program. For a while it seems to be helping. But exercise will not make time stand still. A man has to deal with the fact of aging.

Finally, facing the reality of one's own mortality can be devastating. When we're younger, it is easier to deny the fact that we are going to die. The sunset of life seems so far away. But as we get older, some of our friends die of heart attacks and from cancer. We watch our parents age and die. They remind us that we too will go this way. A man begins to think of how little time is left. It is terribly threatening to feel that life has passed you by and death is just around the corner.

The really disturbing issue underlying a man's experience of change in any of these areas is that his sense of identity is being undermined. He is now thrown into an identity crisis in the middle of his life. A man's career success, his role in the family, his appearance, how he is treated by his company and work associates are all the common sources of identity for him. Some of these involvements have given him a sense of worth and accomplishment. Now things have changed. Who is he now? Is he still worth anything?

The mid-life transition is a time when many men involve themselves with another woman. Most often a middle-aged man will find a younger woman. Since the core of his problem is a shaken identity, he is particularly vulnerable to her flattery. Anything she says about his achievements, how important he is, the fact that he is so young for his age, will be hard to resist for the man in mid-life crisis. The relationship with the younger woman is concrete proof that he, too, is still young, still an appealing personality. The affair is a desperate attempt to deny mortality and to substantiate a man's shifting sense of self-worth.

This is why we have to be especially careful during our middle years. The involvement with another woman can for a time divert a man's attention from the painful emotions of mid-life, but the woman will only be temporary relief, like Novocain injected at the root of an abscessed tooth. If nothing is done to fix the tooth, the pain will return. At best, the affair is a brief detour from real life that will necessarily cause greater pain and tension in the long run. There is nothing worse than standing by helplessly while watching deep pain and loneliness inhabit a man who has lived through the full scope of this disillusionment.

All of us will go through this transition. For some, the struggle to find a renewed sense of identity will be difficult. Some men will not let go of the trapeze bar. They swing back and forth, back and forth. They might even try to return to the platform of their youth. They deny the reality of the changes that are happening in their lives. They cover up with drinking, activities, younger women. But all cover-ups lead to greater despair. We have all seen the lost and confused middle-aged man who thinks that opening his shirt a few buttons and wearing bikini underwear will somehow restore his shattered ego. It is a pitiful sight.

Letting go of the swinging bar is incredibly difficult. There is that gut-wrenching, falling feeling that grips the pit of the stomach. There is the tension of doubt and fear. And when we are afraid we are tempted to do something foolish. We must not. Our faith will save us at this point. Our God is a God of hope. He is the God of our future. When we feel the fear, we can turn to God and avail ourselves of all the resources of the Christian faith to keep moving ahead.

In Christ we can have the courage to honestly explore new opportunities for growth. The mid-life requires acceptance of change, the courage to risk new directions in life, the strength to admit and move beyond our failures and inadequacies. Turn to God and seek his leading and strength. Ask your close friends to help you sort through some of the things you're feeling. And most important, turn toward your wife during this time. She loves you and accepts you more than anyone else. She knows the real you and loves you. She understands you better than anyone else. Her wisdom and support are exactly what you need when you're questioning the meaning of life. Don't isolate yourself from God, your Christian friends (especially other men) or your loving wife.

Change is always painful. But in the case of the mid-life transition, it is clearly more painful to deny reality or to try to cling to the past than it is to face the temporary dislocation of risking a new future. The longer we put off taking those first important steps toward the new life ahead, the harder our lives will become. Reality will finally and destructively overpower any rationalization, shallow pretense or escape behavior.

The rock climber slips his fingertips into a damp crevice in the sheer wall above and begins to shift his weight. The sky diver leaps from the plane and tightens his grip on the ripcord. The trapeze artist swings out, lets go and sails into the void.

Can we trust God with our lives? The Scripture says, "By faith the people passed through the Red Sea as on dry land" (Heb 11:29). The mid-life transition is for every man a personal, mini-Red Sea experience. Egypt is behind, the promised land ahead. Turning back is not an option for the godly man.

Step out in faith. Our God is a God of new life and new beginnings. He will see us through to dry land and place our feet again on solid ground.

Questions for Groups and Individuals

1. Have you witnessed in your family or circle of friends the destructive results of an adulterous relationship? How did you react emotionally?

What did you learn from that experience?

2. What are the factors in your social life, in your particular work situation, in your marriage relationship, or within yourself that you think might make you susceptible to having an affair?

3. The author develops a twelve-step affair process. (pp.89-93) Do these steps ring true to you? Explain.

4. Our society no longer gives us very clear guidelines on what are acceptable and unacceptable ways for men and women to relate to one another. What are some definite, practical limits you think a man might adhere to in relationships with women that could help keep him from situations that might be a temptation for him?

5. Besides taking negative steps to avoid the temptation to adultery, what are positive ways you have found to build your marriage relationship?

6. Choose one practical step you could take right now that would make your marriage stronger.

7. Have you experienced a midlife crisis? How did it affect you? Share any insights you gained that might help others.

5/THE TEMPTATION TO WIELD POWER

The lesser god wants his followers to hug their power to themselves;
if others are as powerful as we, what's the point of having power?
It's only good as long as it puts us above and beyond
our fellow human beings. The true power of the greater God demands
that it be shared. To hug it to ourselves—and say definitely,
"It's mine! It belongs to me!"—is to lose it for the power of the lesser god.

CHERYL FORBES

P ower abuse is an ugly transgression.

I have never forgotten a university professor's calculated use of power of position against his students at my alma mater. This professor taught the only sections of Advanced Composition offered in the English department. If a student wanted to graduate from that university with a major or minor in English, he had to pass this professor's required course. The man was a homosexual, and he used the power inherent in his position against the students, who were particularly vulnerable, in order to satisfy his lust. Every class knew of at least one student who had been consistently pressured, threatened and who had eventually capitulated out of fear. Others who would not be intimidated were sometimes forced to change their major or even leave the school to pursue their educational goals.

A number of us in the department worked for nearly two years on the problem. The professor chose his victims carefully. It was not possible to find anyone who would risk admitting publicly (although several would admit it privately) that he had been forced into a homosexual relationship against his will. But we were able to convince the department head to open up other sections of Advanced Comp taught by different professors. This helped. Because you could choose your professors, the person in question wound up with increasingly smaller classes and fewer sections to teach. I heard some time after I graduated that the man had been compelled by the new arrangement to make positive changes in his teaching approach in order to win students to his classes and save his job.

Nietzsche is attributed with the saying, "Basic to the human personality is the will to power." He was right. And we might add an inductive truth, "Basic to the structure of all human institutions is the will to power." Every aspect of our society—business, politics, education, religion, marriage and family—operates largely on the basis of power.

There are negative and destructive powers. And there are positive and creative powers. The Christian has to distinguish between the two and choose the latter. Are you using power to promote yourself without regard for others? Or are you, as you should be, using power to promote others without regard for yourself? How are you known by others? Is your lifestyle marked by loving action toward those around you? Or are you known more for your use of the power play to get your way in the world? True, it is not always easy to discern whether we are acting properly. There are muddy waters in the river of power. It always helps to remember the teaching and lifestyle of Jesus when we consider the topic of power and its appropriate use.

Mark describes in detail in his gospel the story of James and John coming to Jesus with a request. They wanted the Lord to allow one of them to sit at his right and one at his left when he achieved his glory (Mk 10:35-45). It is a compelling story. When the other disciples hear of the request they are immediately angered. It is apparent that their irritation does not spring from righteous motives. Each one is secretly convinced that he is the most deserving of the number-one spot ahead of the rest. James and John and all of the other disciples appear to be primarily interested in themselves and how they can put themselves in a favorable position through the use of power. We know that they often argued with one another about who was the greatest (Mk 9:34).

Jesus lovingly calls them to himself and makes several important points about power and position. He says, "You know that those who are regarded as rulers of the Gentiles lord it over them, and their high officials exercise authority over them. Not so with you" (Mk 10:42-43). He shows them that there are two distinct styles of leadership, the world's style and the kingdom's style. He says the rulers of the world lord it over their subjects, dominating them through power. But Jesus is quick to point out that it must not be this way in the kingdom of God. He goes on to say, "Instead, whoever wants to be great among you must be your servant, and whoever wants to be first must be slave of all" (vv. 43-44). The true mark of kingdom leadership is servanthood, not title, position or the coercive use of power. The kingdom leader following the example of Christ has to be willing to be last for the sake of all, actually the "slave" of all.

Jesus makes his life-purpose and lifestyle the model for kingdom leadership. He says, "For even the Son of Man did not come to be served, but to serve, and to give his life as a ransom for many" (vv. 45). We immediately think of Philippians 2 in this regard. Jesus emptied himself, took on the form of a slave. Of what did he empty himself? The glory of Heaven. Yes, and power!

Jesus was a master of the proper use of power. He sensitively sought to empower others with the means to effectively manage their lives under God. Jesus did not use power against others to promote himself or his causes, but demonstrated with his life that the power of authentic love empowers others to grow to the fullness of all they were meant to be. Jesus always refused to take advantage of another's weaknesses. Instead, he encouraged strengths and acted in the power of love to empower others to follow his loving example.

Yes, there were times when Jesus used aggressive, physical power. Clearing the temple was one of those times. But keep in mind the motive behind his use of physical power. Is it selfish? Or is the power aimed toward others, toward their good, helping them to see something they need to see and to move beyond where they are to something better? Even physical power can be used with the best interests of others in mind. There is a proper place for the righteous use of physical power just as there is a proper place for righteous anger. Jesus often came against the Pharisees with force. But again, it was not for selfish gain and never to exploit them in any way. Jesus' motives were always rooted and grounded in love for those he confronted.

I have become convinced that we cannot have it both ways. Love and worldly power are like a lamb and a lion; they will not lie down together. What will we choose? Will we operate from a worldly power base? Or will we be rooted and grounded in kingdom love?

Christians must say no to the temptation to use manipulative or coercive power to further themselves or their selfish ends. Jesus said we were to follow his example of kingdom leadership. Then he gave us a picture of this unusual leadership style. He took the basin and towel and knelt to wash the feet of his disciples. He said, "Now that I, your Lord and Teacher, have washed your feet, you also should wash one another's feet. I have set you an example that you should do as I have done for you" (Jn 13:14-15).

Christian men are to be servants, footwashers, leaders in love in the church, their businesses, their families and in the world. What will this kind of behavior look like? How can we resist the temptation to wield power? What is the cost of Christlike commitment in this area? And are we willing to pay the price?

Worldly Power in the Church

No biblical writer addresses the topic of abuse of power in the church more directly than James. He will not tolerate favoritism shown to the rich and influential (2:1-13). He attacks the sham of a faith of words alone with no deeds, describing the use of empty words as an attempt to sound righteous and, without authentic Christian living, to position oneself in a place of power in the church (2:14-26). James shows convincingly that evil power is unleashed in the church through the tongue (3:1-12). Christian teachers have to be very careful not to use their power-filled gift for their own ends (3:1-2). And he shows that even slander is a form of power abuse because a person who slanders another places himself in the position of God the Judge, above the law (3:11-12). The person who boasts about his future similarly sins by taking the position of God, thinking somehow that he is all-powerful to do what he wills with his life and work (3:13-16).

If we show favoritism to the powerful, or expect to be shown favoritism because we are powerful, we sin. The world invades the church with power. A friend of mine told me a story of something that happened at the Bel Aire Presbyterian Church one morning. When in attendance, Governor Ronald Reagan and Nancy usually sat in the same two seats just off the center aisle about two-thirds of the way into the sanctuary. On this particular morning the governor and his wife were late and by the time they got there, two college students had occupied those seats. An usher came down the aisle and asked the students if they would take different seats off to the side. They moved, and

Ron and Nancy were brought in and seated. To his credit, Pastor Don Moomau got up from his place in the chancel, walked down and over to the college students and said, "As long as I am pastor of this church, that will never happen to you again." Favoritism recognizes worldly position and power. It has no place in the church.

Another kind of political power used in the church is the manipulative power of the group that works behind the scenes to promote or prevent some movement in the church. A well-known pastor in a church in Washington, D.C., told me that his congregation divides into such factions each year to campaign for representatives to be elected to the board of elders. Decisions in the church about programs, new directions, personnel, should not be made on the basis of power groups who engage in power politics. Church life should be governed by prayerful and wise decisions that have the opportunity of full process in the leadership structure of the church. Each of us has an obligation to work toward discerning the godly option through loving and open study, discussion and prayer. We should refuse to participate in any faction or to allow factions to perpetuate their opinions by worldly methods of influence through power.

Preachers and teachers will need to be extremely careful, as James indicates in his letter. Those who are gifted by God as teachers will come to the place where they recognize the power in what they do. The temptation will be to use this power for selfish rather than godly ends. The end of Jim Jones's ministry in the jungle of Guyana reminds us all of the tragedy of gifts of power turned toward the sinful self. We can be guilty of using the speaking gift to build ourselves up in the eyes of others. We can be tempted to give people what they want instead of what we believe God would want us to do. I have often thought of what a tremendous burden it must be to be "the" preaching minister at the Crystal Cathedral or on other nationally broadcast programs. Each week you would be tempted to look at a message from the point of view of how much money it generated for the ministry. The temptation would be to duplicate in style and content messages that are big sellers.

We who teach and speak on a smaller scale have the same temptations. The sermon can be used to get what we want, to pump up the building campaign or the stewardship drive, to get more Sunday-school teachers, or to make the congregation more receptive to giving a much-needed raise. Another temptation for preachers and teachers is to begin to enjoy standing in the place of God in the lives of those we teach. We would do well to remember that we too stand under God's Word, in his forgiveness, and we are one with our congregations in this respect. We should come to teaching and preaching with much prayer and confession so we will not use this power for our own ends.

James gets after those whose faith is a show of words in the same way Jesus got after the Pharisees. The Pharisees wore religious clothes, spoke religious jargon and practiced external shows of religious habit—fasting, praying, making vows. They loved to hold positions, to be exalted by those around them, to have influence in religious matters. Jesus saw through this hypocrisy. He said, "Be careful not to do your 'acts of righteousness' before men, to be seen by them. . . . When you give to the needy, do not announce it with trumpets, as the hypocrites do in the synagogues and on the streets, to be honored by men. . . . When you pray, do not be like the hypocrites, for they love to pray standing in the synagogues and on the street corners to be seen by men. I tell you the truth, they have received their reward in full" (Mt 6:1-5). The Pharisees received what they were looking for, human approval. But they would receive no more.

Why do we seek high visibility? Why do we want to look religious? To hunger for position reveals our desire to have and wield power. Jesus had heroes. We all remember them—the humble sinner who prayed in anguish that he might be forgiven, the widow who brought everything she had and put it in the offering, the woman who washed his feet with her tears and wiped them with her hair.

How different we are from Jesus. I have heard myself say to others, "He (or she) would make a great Christian." I have looked at attractiveness and worldly influence, the external trappings of power and have judged one person more worthy of the gospel than another. The strategy some campus groups have of winning the influential people in an area falls perilously close to this kind of favoritism. We appear to believe that God needs people of worldly power and influence to accomplish his work in the world.

In *Everyday Evangelism* I wrote about the abuse of power of Christian organizations that use manipulative techniques to raise funds to build Christian empires. Oral Roberts recently told his supporters that God would take him home if he did not raise $8 million for medical missionary scholarships. He raised the eight million, but now appears to have used the money for everything but the needed scholarships. It's the old shell game. We should be ashamed of ourselves. What do churches do when they get in trouble financially? It is certainly better for Christian organizations to fold than to use the power methods of the world to stay afloat.

Since I wrote *Everyday Evangelism,* things have gotten worse rather than better. It has been seen that Jim and Tammy Bakker, Jimmy Swaggart and others less prominent have used their power of position to gain the world for themselves. Peter Popoff, a popular faith healer, was discovered wearing a radio receiver through which he could hear his wife reading to him from backstage personal information from cards handed in by the audience. For years he has astonished followers with an uncanny awareness of details of their personal lives, like doctors' names, phone numbers and addresses, the history of and factual information about their illnesses. These are just a few examples of how the use of the manipulative powers of this world has invaded contemporary Christianity. We need to be on guard. We are all vulnerable.

Our evangelism can become tainted by manipulative power. Even as a believer, I have fallen prey to the efforts of well-meaning brothers and sisters who for one reason or another did not believe I was Christian enough to suit them. Once I attended a wedding at a conservative congregation in Boulder. As members of that church came up and talked with me, I could tell that everything they asked had an edge to it. They worked feverishly to find out who I was and what I believed and wasted no time in cornering me and testing me with biblical verses they had been taught to see in just one way. In this kind of fellowship they ought to read you your rights as you come in the door—everything you do or say may be used against you.

Jesus refused to use worldly power to achieve his ends. Satan's temptation of Jesus in the wilderness was an attempt to get the Lord to use power to advance himself. Jesus knew the only power that would achieve lasting work for his father was the power of loving sacrifice seen most clearly in the cross.

When we approach our neighbors with the gospel, our approach should demonstrate our love for them. Whether we are talking with them about Christ, or giving them a cup of water in his name, they should not feel attacked or manipulated. Judie and I have been invited to dinner by friends only to find out that they really wanted to talk with us about becoming Amway distributors in their "family" tree. It is a disheartening experience to discover that a person who has reached out to you with a caring gesture really had a selfish motivation. Many Christians use this kind of manipulation to attempt to lead those around them to Christ. But coercive technique will not get the job done. Only love will bear lasting fruit for the kingdom.

Sometimes we even exert the power of self-will in our prayers. James writes: "You do not have, because you do not ask God. When you ask, you do not receive, because you ask with the wrong motives, that you may spend what you get on your pleasures" (Jas 4:2-3). Yes, there is power in prayer. But it can be twisted power, a subtle attempt to manipulate God into granting the selfish desires of a heart turned toward the world. The power and presence of God in prayer can free us from our yearnings to gain something for ourselves. Instead of foolishly trying to obtain through prayer those things that would not be good for us, we should be praying for his transforming power to renew our minds and fill our hearts with love for the character and purposes of Christ. It is always the mark of earthly power that it aims at achieving some selfish end or achieving some true good wrongly.

James says that "worldly" wisdom—the wisdom of power, bitter envy and selfish ambition—will bring disorder and every kind of evil practice into the church (Jas 3:16). This is true because there can be no harmony when people seek the satisfaction of their selfish ends. In contrast to the world's way James says: "But the wisdom that comes from heaven is first of all pure; then peace loving, considerate, submissive, full of mercy and good fruit, impartial and sincere. Peacemakers who sow in peace raise a harvest of righteousness" (Jas 3:17-18).

Wisdom is a godly heart applied to life's choices. It is a heart that looks for God and yearns for his way in every decision, every step forward and every action toward others, courageously refusing to use manipulative power to capture something for itself.

Power in the Christian Family

Relationships in the Christian family are to be love-based rather than power-based. It is a great irony that the passage written by the apostle Paul to abrogate the secular and Jewish tradition of the absolute power and dominance of the man is often used today to try to give this kind of unqualified power back to the man. It might be good to stop here and reread Ephesians 5:21-33 if you have not reviewed the passage recently. Paul's purpose throughout this whole chapter is to describe the behaviors of love and respect that should characterize all relationships, husbands and wives, parents and children, even slaves and masters. His word of love is penetrating and revolutionary. Paul is proposing here a radical, liberating view.

First Paul spells out for wives the part they are to play in the loving interaction of mutual submission in a marriage. He writes: "Wives, submit to your husbands as to the Lord. For the husband is the head of the wife as Christ is the head of the church, his body, of which he is the Savior" (Eph 5:22-23). It is important to notice first that Paul addresses the wives directly. If Paul had wanted to express this in the customary manner of his times he would have written instead, "Husbands, make your wives submit to you." In Jewish law, the woman was a thing, not a person. But Paul addresses the women of the church as individuals capable of making their own decisions regarding such important matters as their style of relating in marriage. Then in another radical shift from accepted practice, Paul asks wives to defer in love to their husbands alone. Women were expected to be subservient and obedient to all men. Paul's manner of speaking directly to the women in the church would be a shocking and disturbing departure from cultural bias for the conventional first-century man.

This submission Paul asks for from Christian women is defined and qualified by the concept of Christ's headship of the church. Remember what his headship means and the emphasis Paul is placing on it in this passage. Christ loved the church so much that he would die for her, give his life for the church, so that the church could share in every blessing. Paul makes this meaning clear when he writes, "Husbands, love your wives, just as Christ loved the church and gave himself up for her" (Eph 5:25).

This is agape in action. Agape is totally selfless, other-centered love. It is the love that characterizes the love of Christ for the Father, the love of God for men and women. Husbands are to love their wives with this kind of selfless love. The husband's role in mutual submission is to give over his cultural right to dominate his wife and to choose to love her sacrificially. The wife is asked to yield her rights and powers in love to a husband who yields his rights and powers in love to her. This is the mutual submission at which Paul aims that if practiced will lead to success in marriage (Eph 5:21).

Throughout the passage Paul refuses to picture or use in describing the man's role any of the readily available Greek terms for leader, ruler or authority. Paul's chosen term is *head*. In the Greek this term means "source." It is not a term used in the biblical material to picture a dominant authority figure. Certainly Christ has authority in our lives. And we are to be obedient to his rightful authority. There is no question about this. But to make authority central in this passage is to misread Paul's intent and take his analogy too far. Paul's emphasis is carefully chosen. He focuses on the power of agape in headship, not on the power of authority. Paul is thoroughly consistent here with his use of the image of Christ as head earlier in Ephesians 4:15-16. These verses also describe relationships that grow in quality and strength because they are joined and held together by sacrificial love. Christ's headship is pictured in this book as one of love and nurture, not control, dominance or suppression.

The submission of a wife to her husband is a submission of grace to a man who demonstrates daily that he loves her so much that he would die for her. She is not being told here to be obedient to her husband. There is no New Testament verse that describes the relationship of the wife to the husband as one characterized by obedience. But she is being asked to yield her powers to her husband who has already yielded his powers to her. It is love, not control, that is the issue. John Stott describes the mutual submission in this way. He writes: "Submission is something quite different from obedience. It is a voluntary self-giving to a lover whose responsibility is defined in terms of constructive care; it is love's response to love."[1]

A woman has great power. We have talked in chapter three about her deep inner security, her ability to live independently, her power in the family and society, and her skillful, natural strengths in the relational dimensions of life. She also has tremendous sexual power that could be used to dominate and control men. But Paul asks the woman to submit her powers in love to create a mutually responsive relationship of care, respect and self-sacrifice after the model of Christ and the church.

The men of Paul's day were enculturated with Jewish law and a societal view that saw women as nothing. The man was expected to demand, dominate, use women at will, even physically abuse and sexually mistreat women. Paul takes an incredible giant leap forward in this passage. He tells men to submit their Jewish and pagan rights of position to their wives and to view the marriage relationship as a mutual interplay of sacrificial love and good will. The man is told to model the selfless love of Christ toward his wife and in his family.

The man today who asks "Who is the head of the house?" in order to establish himself as the authority figure in the marriage relationship is far from a biblical understanding on this subject. He is concerned with his rights, his position. He wants the same thing that James and John wanted when they asked Jesus for the positions on the right and left of him in his glory. Jesus would not condone this kind of self-seeking hunger for power and authority. He showed that concern for rights and position are the way of the world, not of the kingdom. In the

Ephesian passage we have studied, Paul aligns himself with Jesus in this matter. As we grow in Christ, there should be a continually diminishing concern for our rights in the Christian marriage relationship. The focus is to be on love, mutual respect, mutual concern for Christlikeness and the behaviors of grace.

To learn what it means in a practical way to love your wife as Christ loved the church and to build the marriage relationship in love rather than in worldly power, read and study everything Paul says in Ephesians four and five about relationships in the body of Christ. These truths apply to all relationships and are especially fruitful if incorporated into your marriage and family life.

Paul is also concerned with right relationships with children. He writes, "Fathers, do not exasperate your children; instead, bring them up in the training and instruction of the Lord" (Eph 6:4). A parallel passage in Colossians reads, "Fathers, do not embitter your children, or they will become discouraged" (Col 3:21). My experience has shown me that a child's relationship with his father is key to his spiritual development. Children who have been exasperated, embittered and discouraged because of their relationship with their fathers often find it nearly impossible to develop a healthy relationship with God.

The key to positive parenting with positive results is found in the phrase "bring them up in the training and instruction of the Lord." Our parenting style should be a godly style modeled after the manner in which God loves and builds us in the Christian life. If we emphasize power in our childrearing and de-emphasize love, our children will always struggle with the question of how they are to respond to authority in their lives. If we are demanding and abusive, we will exasperate our children and drive them far from us, and perhaps far from God.

Jesus modeled love and forgiveness. It is the core of the gospel. He did not demand perfect behavior before he would accept us. As a matter of fact, he gave his life for us while we were far from him, in the deepest need.

Children will accept our firm discipline if they know that we love them. In fact, discipline is a necessary component of love; God disciplines us. But what we have to remember is that God's discipline is always for our growth and development. We accept discipline because we have a deep sense of God's love for us and his justice. We trust him. He is fair. He is forgiving. He will hold us accountable, but he does not demean us, make fun of our inadequacies, use our weaknesses against us, or play games with our feelings about ourselves. Even as he disciplines us, he holds us lovingly to himself.

Our relationship with our children should be characterized by consistent and loving affirmation and consistent and loving discipline and instruction. The fruit of the Spirit can guide us in giving ourselves to our kids in a Christlike way. Our interaction in love, joy, peace, patience, kindness, goodness, faithfulness, gentleness and self-control will produce children of grace and love rather than broken children, exasperated and deeply wounded by the severe wielding of abusive power.

Pay particular attention as a husband or father to the power of the affirmative word. Our words have tremendous power to build up or to tear down. The apostle Paul told early Christians to stop saying the things that diminish others and to concentrate instead on speaking words of encouragement that empower others for growth. He writes, "Do not let any unwholesome talk come out of your mouths, but only what is helpful for building others up according to their needs, that it may benefit those who listen" (Eph 4:29). In the family our aim is to try to catch our kids doing something good so we can affirm them. Affirmation puts the power of love to work in another's life.

Encouraging our wives is equally important. A sad memory I have is of a conversation I once had with a woman who was struggling in her marriage. She shared that she felt so insecure and weak that she did not know if she was going to make it. She told me that if her husband would just encourage her it would make such a difference. I asked if she had shared this need with him. She said she asked him once if he would tell her when she did something right. He responded by saying, "When you do something right, I'll tell you!" They had been married over twenty-five years. She could not remember one time that he had affirmed or encouraged her in any way.

I wish every family had a tape recording system that traced the quality of conversation in the home. It would be good to be able to listen to our conversations with one another and to measure whether we are spending most of our time in "un-wholesome talk" or if we are "building others up according to their needs." We must think before we speak: "Am I building my wife up with this remark? Or am I tearing her down? Am I building my son up? Or my daughter? Or am I tearing them down?" In our families and with others around us we often make the mistake of emphasizing the negative. But if we continually focus on the weaknesses of another, the negative focus will tear that person down. If we affirm the positive, it produces a strong foundation from which we can build new strengths. Nothing is accomplished over the long haul by majoring on the problems and negatives in another person's life.

I remember reading a short fable about a school for animals. They adopted a curriculum of running, climbing, swimming and flying. All the animals had to work in all the subjects. The duck was making fine grades in swimming, but not doing well in running. In order to improve, he had to cut back on swimming and stay after school to work on running. Soon his webbed feet were badly torn up, sore and bruised. Now his grades in swimming went down as well. The rabbit started at the top of the class in running, but developed some nervous twitching in the leg muscles because of so much makeup work in swimming. His teacher kept piling on the swimming lessons, and in the end the rabbit became as mediocre in running as he was in swimming. The squirrel was excellent in climbing, but terrible at flying. Flying class was especially tiring for the squirrel because the flying teacher made him start from the ground with all his flying exercises. Soon he was too exhausted to climb.

What a tremendous difference it will make if we will form a regular habit of seeing the positive, focusing on the strengths of those we care about and affirming them in the good they do. A kind word, a written recognition of a job well done, even a physical touch to communicate positive feelings are the powers that build others up in love.

Paul asks us to get rid of all "bitterness, rage and anger, brawling and slander, along with every form of malice" (Eph 4:31). He entreats us to be "kind and compassionate to one another, forgiving each other, just as in Christ God forgave you" (v. 32). The first list of behaviors are the behaviors of division and destruction. They will not build, but are the powers that tear down relationships and demean those who are the recipients of the actions of negative power. The second list names the behaviors of positive power. They are the actions of affirmation and acceptance that build the kingdom of God. Christ can develop these qualities in us as fathers and husbands. We should seek wisdom and love and pray that God will break all our selfish and prideful desires for omnipotence.

Power in the Business World

To control power in the business world is an awesome task for the Christian. Ego power, money power, power of position and sexual power rule the workplace. The temptation will be to fight fire with fire. Yet, if the Spirit lives within us, we cannot help but be haunted by the teachings of Jesus in this area. When we wield power, we have a nagging feeling in the pit of our stomachs. Jesus would not have acted in the same way. He would have turned the other cheek. "But," you may ask, "how can we get ahead of the Japanese by turning the other cheek?"

Let's think first about the abuses of power on the relational level. Life can be tough for you if you work for people who have a need to control and who use power against you. They may be trying to compensate for feelings of insecurity, low self-esteem. Perhaps they wield power because their supervisors demand decisive action and have little concern for human dimensions in the workplace. Or they have lived a life without power and now do not know how to live with it. Whatever is behind this kind of driving, controlling personality, working for such persons will be emotionally draining.

A close friend of mine has worked with a petty, control-oriented person for several years. It has been a struggle from day one. My friend is supposed to be office manager in this medium-sized business. That's the title on the job description, and the position for which he was hired. But the partner and owner he works for feels uncomfortable if anything happens without his involvement. There is no question that my friend is competent to manage the office. The owner travels often and takes a long vacation each year. The office runs well and smoothly in his absence. But when the owner is in the office, he arbitrarily overturns decisions my friend has made, even when they are clearly in line with policies and procedures the owner himself has communicated in writing. He cannot allow someone else to make a decision without his approval, even if it is clearly within guidelines he has developed. He uses veto power if he has not participated in the decision, even if it is so small as deciding how much soda should be ordered for the pop machine.

I have followed my friend's problem carefully for several years. My initial instincts were to counsel him to quit and work somewhere else where he had the freedom to function at the high level of his abilities. But now I think that might have been the wrong advice in this case. My friend chose to stay because he felt God might have a reason for him to be there. At first he saw that he could promote job satisfaction for others in the office by affirming them and caring about them and allowing them the freedom of responsibility in their areas of expertise that he himself was denied. He also saw that his model of selflessness in the face of pressures and pettiness from the boss was having a positive effect on the office. My friend was not making a big deal out of it. He refused to engage in any kind of gossip or to position himself against his supervisor. He simply tried as much as was possible to live in a pressure-cooker situation while relying on God for patience and a proper attitude. His behavior brought the respect of many of those who worked for him, and he began to have influence in their personal lives.

At first one young woman from the office visited his church. In time she recommitted her life to Christ and became an active member involved in music ministry. Another young woman asked if he would help her and her boyfriend work through some difficult personal problems. They wanted to get married, but were fighting constantly. He met with them as a friend to sort through some of the difficulties they were having, and he helped them to get involved with a premarriage class in the church. He has had many other opportunities to minister on a personal level because of the manner in which he lovingly managed others while he himself was badgered from above.

My friend was satisfied that God had a purpose for him in that work situation. He was growing in Christ. He was powerless to affect the personal style of his boss, but he did have the power to choose a different style with those he supervised. His godly choices stood out against the backdrop of his boss's selfish and worldly motivations. He was effective for Christ because he was able to turn the other cheek, refusing to retaliate or to act precipitately to improve his situation.

This is a difficult road. It is tough to consider that God may want you in a position of powerlessness because he has work to do through you. It goes against our nature. It is unmanly. It even seems anti-American because we believe in fixing situations quickly if they are not satisfying to us. But godly patience and wisdom are needed for us to know why God has placed us where we are. God often works best through our personal powerlessness.

There is also a great temptation to try to promote ourselves through the use of power. We all know how it works. We can take credit for things that someone else has done. We can use information we have gathered against others who might be competing with us for position on the corporate ladder. There are opportunities to set up people in our work situations so they will owe us a favor if we ever need it. And we all know people who "suck up" and "kick down." It's all part of the game.

On the other hand the Christian man's life goal is to serve God, not to climb the corporate ladder. Jesus said to his followers, "If anyone would come after me, he must deny himself and take up his cross and follow me" (Mt 16:24). Can a man on a cross have a career path? If Christianity means anything at all, it means turning away from our selfish motivations and considering how our lives, our decisions, our actions can serve the good of God and his purposes in the world.

If we sit in the seat of power in our workplace, there are numerous ways we can choose to use our power for the good of others. First, our decisions regarding those we employ should be fair. We can demonstrate our real concern for those who work for us by being inclusive, willing to listen, working to enhance job performance by giving opportunities for creative decision-making and real responsibility. Those who work for us should not feel that they are only important to us because of the profit margin they can produce, that we are only using them to make money. Of course, a company has to make money to stay in business. But if we make money at the expense of the humanity of our employees, how can we claim to be followers of Christ?

Fairness will mean that we promote employees on the basis of performance, giftedness and personal qualities suited for a particular position. It is not right to promote—or refuse to promote—on the basis of sexual or racial preference. We will use our positions to ensure that this kind of bias does not enter into decisions about promotion or benefits or salary increases.

Christian men today have a particularly difficult challenge to face in regard to treatment of women in the workplace. Capable, creative, skillful women have entered the work force and still have to deal almost daily with sexual discrimination in varying degrees. The Christian man will be a leader in setting the standards of the future for salary, promotions and acceptable working conditions for women. Men complain about women using their sexuality to gain promotions and favors. And men are irritated that attractive women can have an advantage over them. But the truth is that men exercise the real power advantage in the workplace. They have protected their own rights, while keeping talented women frozen at a particular level, so they will not be a threat to the male-dominated system that is well in place.

Christian men should be at the forefront in creating an equitable work situation for all. Men who work to fairly promote qualified women will also help to break the traditional pattern of forcing women to use their sexual power as a way to gain recognition and promotion. Women should be free to be themselves, to creatively concentrate on their work. No one should have to try to work well while having to manage the nagging bitterness that creeps in when one is under the constant pressure of being unfairly treated.

Truth and honesty in business is another power issue. Lies are manipulative powers used to grab something for ourselves.

Lies occur in business to control reality for some selfish end. We want something for ourselves, or we do not want something to happen to us, so we lie. We deny our part in something to save ourselves. Or we color the truth to make a deal and secure something for ourselves. Behind both behaviors lies our fear and insecurity, our lack of trust in God. If we trusted God, we would tell the truth.

A man who teaches with me regularly has struggled in his business. God has taught him many things over these past few years. He told me at lunch the other day that he is learning to ask the right questions. In relation to business deals he asks himself what he is afraid to tell the other person. And when he identifies the items he feels like holding back from someone, he forces himself to share those things and trusts God for the outcome. He also is careful to ask his lawyer every pertinent question regarding a business transaction. He says the temptation is to not ask so you can plead ignorance later when the trouble starts.

Convenient memory is another honesty problem. We remember things the way we want to remember them. We rearrange reality for our convenience. It is important to remember when some problem occurs that there are always two sides to every story and that we are partially at fault. Such wisdom will help greatly in our dealings with others.

There are many professions today in which you might benefit financially from subtle deceptions. It is often in his best economic self-interest for a lawyer to create conflict. The more questions and problems that come up in a deal, the more work it is for the lawyers to untangle the knots. The lawyers are the only ones who make out in many business deals and family squabbles. Dentists and doctors have the same ethical dimensions to their work. I remember one dentist prescribing several thousand dollars' worth of work for my wife. We got a second opinion and received successful treatment for less than five hundred dollars. A doctor can recommend a more expensive operation, just to be sure. Planned obsolescence would be an equivalent type of integrity issue in industry.

Lies in business are a power manipulation because they do not allow others to freely interact with us. We are controlling them with our lies. Don't rationalize away the real state of affairs just to make a profit or save your pride. Be a man of integrity in your business and your dealings with others.

Other powers that can be abused in the business world include the power of manipulative advertising, the power of the hard sell, the power of the sheer-force take-over, the power of monopoly and price fixing, and the power of all business decisions which ignore or diminish humanity, oppressing men and women out of greed and the desire for selfish gain. There isn't the time or space to develop each of these topics in this single chapter on power. The significant point of challenge for us here is to recognize as sin the use of all power that aims at getting and grabbing something for ourselves at the expense of others.

The tough thing—if we are serious about our Christian commitment—will be to choose against power when we recognize that we have slipped over into its world of control, manipulation and dominance. Power in the world is like a river that carries us along. If we don't fight it, things appear to go pretty smoothly, at least on the surface. When we try to swim against the stream, we really find out what we're up against.

What will you do now that you have read this material, and the thought has occurred to you that the ads for your new product line are not completely honest, that they present the best side of things, or appeal in a powerful and manipulative way only to the emotions? Will you choose to advertise differently? Advertising can be good and true. Those of us who claim to belong to Christ have an obligation to consider the proper use of power in advertising.

And what will you do the next time you know you could push others into making purchases even though they are not really ready to buy? Will you push? Or will you let the deal develop naturally? Will you give the potential buyer the space to consider whether the deal is right, even though your competition does not share your moral perspective? Where does trusting God come into our dealings in the competitive world of work? Is it up to us to push? Closing a deal and forcing a deal are quite different. Where is our biblical precedent for forcing closure?

And how will you maintain Christian advocacy for the poor and exploited and powerless from your present position in a multinational corporation? It is certainly not enough to sit back and say "there is nothing I can do when my chemical corporation decides to drastically cut its safety budget and standards for its new plant in India." It is not enough to claim powerlessness when my corporation buys up huge segments of tillable land in Guatemala to grow coffee for export to Europe and the United States, not when that land could and should be used to grow food for its own people. What will we do? How will our powerful corporations be held accountable?

It is easy to rationalize in this area. Even if we own a small business we have the power to make decisions that will promote God's general will or deter it. We make decisions daily that speak of the view we hold toward people who have been created by God, and toward his created environment. We have the power to treat people and God's earth in ways that model faith, trust and our Christian value perspective, or to make decisions rooted in self-concern, fear or greed. If we spend more time reading our trade journals than reading the Bible, we can quickly lose our perspective. Trade journals are written to promote our industry. They will not ask the tough questions about product and policy that need to be asked. We can count on the Holy Spirit, though, to keep us dealing with the right issues if we will choose to open our hearts and minds to the power of the Spirit working through God's Word. We can trust God to help us to see how his truth is real and applicable to our lives today.

I can hear the protests. Most of them really come down to the question of whether it is possible to be successful in business if we really do things right. I will grant that it is extraordinarily difficult. But I will not agree that it is impossible. There are many true stories of Christian men and women who have accomplished what appeared to be the impossible by having the courage to risk pointing out that a decision or practice is wrong. Some have personally and quietly refused to obey corporate edicts that were clearly against biblical norms and have had enormous impact by standing for God. Some have done the same and been fired. Some have had to quit their jobs in order to make clear something that has been hidden or ignored.

No, there are no guarantees. God has not promised us that if we choose to live out our Christian commitment in the marketplace we will be able to keep our present jobs. But we will keep our integrity. And we might make a real difference where we are by living in the power of powerlessness after the model of Christ. There is really no alternative to living faithfully. Jesus cuts to the heart of the matter in Matthew 16:26 when he says, "What good will it be for a man if he gains the whole world, yet forfeits his soul?"

The Power of God for Good

In the church power should be used to build the community of the faithful. The goal for God's new society is "to prepare God's people for works of service, so that the body of Christ may be built up until we all reach unity in the faith and in the knowledge of the Son of God and become mature, attaining to the whole measure of the fullness of Christ" (Eph 4:12-13). We choose to give ourselves to God to be used powerfully by him for the good of Christian community.

In the family, too, power is to be used to build up rather than tear down. The power of communication will overcome isolation; the power of affirmation will build self-esteem; the power of forgiveness will develop unity in love and create a permission-giving atmosphere in which family members will feel free to risk and free to admit their need to grow and become.

Positive power in business will diminish competition and promote corporate community and team consciousness. Emphasis can be placed on the significance of individual gifts used for the good of all. True responsibility will lead to creative contribution in the workplace. The power of moral integrity will help corporations and individuals to gain a vision for building something beyond themselves. A moral foundation is needed if we are ever to have hope that decisions will really be made for the good of human community.

The Power of Prayer

In this power struggle we battle against spiritual forces. To quote Paul again: "Finally, be strong in the Lord and in his mighty power. Put on the full armor of God so that you can take your stand against the devil's schemes. For our struggle is not against flesh and blood, but against the rulers, against the authorities, against the powers of this dark world and against the spiritual forces of evil in the heavenly realms" (Eph 6:10-12).

This is a war that cannot be won with human effort alone. We need the full armor of God to overcome the subtle and often-overwhelming temptations of the world in this area of power. We need the belt of truth, the breastplate of righteousness, the shield of faith, the helmet of salvation, the sword of the Spirit. But above all, we must be men of prayer. Paul says: "Pray in the Spirit on all occasions with all kinds of prayers and requests. With this in mind, be alert and always keep on praying for all the saints" (Eph 6:18).

Prayer is our ultimate power against the powers of this world.

The praying man stands with the forces of God against the spiritual powers of evil in the heavenly realms. Great men of the Bible were not powerful because of their human wisdom, their worldly resources, their natural talents, but because they prayed (Gen 32:9-21; 1 Kings 17:1; Neh 1:5; Eph 1:15-16; Mk 1:35). And their earnest prayers in the Spirit commanded the creative power of the living God. The man in prayer has a legitimate hope that in Christ he will gain power over power.

Questions for Groups and Individuals

1. What is power? Give examples from your experience of power being used well and power being abused.

2. Give examples of how you have seen various kinds of power being exercised in your workplace, your family or your church.

3. In what setting do you think it is the most tempting to wield power in a way that is contrary to God's will? Why?

4. In this chapter the author asks the rhetorical question "Does a man on a cross have a career path?" (p. 128) What do you think he is getting at with this question? How would you answer the question?

5. What are some particularly difficult temptations to power that confront a Christian in the business world today? What have you personally found to be the hardest temptation to handle?

6. The author suggests that we "might make a real difference where we are by living in the power of powerlessness after the model of Christ." (p. 133) Can you think of a specific and practical way this could apply to how you should use power in your present circumstances?

6/THE TEMPTATION TO LOVE MONEY

Watch out!
Be on your guard against all kinds of greed;
a man's life does not consist in the
abundance of his possessions.
JESUS, LUKE 12:15

The love of money is the root of all evil.
PAUL, 1 TIMOTHY 6:10

Money is not the root of all evil. The love of money is. Money can become our god. Once our love of money elevates it to this supreme position in our lives, evil will naturally result. We lose all perspective. The power of the world captures us. Nothing will stand in our way—not friends, not family, not even God. Money may be our most difficult obsession. No concept or commodity is more deeply rooted in and driven by our emotional needs. Nothing in the world today is more available, acceptable and heavily promoted. And all the promotion is positive. This is different from other obsessions that may captivate us.

We may struggle with overeating; food is plentiful in America and available in exquisite variety, but we have some help from society to beat our gluttony. There is media pressure against overeating. We know about the health problems that result. We know that being fat is not a generally accepted look today.

Alcohol abuse is similar. Alcohol is widely available in numerous forms. Like food, it is attractively advertised. There is also immense pressure from society to manage drinking. Everyone knows the health hazards associated with alcohol. Everyone knows the potential harm of drinking and driving, both to the drunk driver and to those he may injure or kill. Everyone knows how alcoholism can destroy a man's family, diminish his work, turn him into an emotional cripple. Alcohol is available, but our society has turned against it and provides help by making known its harmful side.

But there is no media campaign to help us control our consumptive materialism and manage our lust for money. A "Manage Your Lust for Money" campaign would have to attack our accepted lifestyle, our emotional needs related to money, our receptivity to advertising that drives our wild consumerism, our credit-based economy, our lack of financial management skills, our tendency toward impulse buying and our failure to approach finances with intentionality that will help guide us toward a proper use of our God-given resources.

Can Money Make You Happy?

There are two mirages that live in the American mind relating to money. I call them mirages because they are concepts that seem substantial but are really empty. They are like the shimmering image of a pool of water we might see ahead on the highway. It looks real as you drive toward it. Then, just before you reach the spot, the image vanishes. With money, too, reality is often vastly different from the image that is projected by the media and captures our imaginations.

The first deception that has captivated the American mind is the "money is the key to happiness" mirage. There are numerous aspects to this mirage along these lines: Money can obtain for you the ultimate security you desire both for you and for your family. Money will make you free and independent. Money will give you power over others. Money brings you respect. All those who have given you grief will whistle a different tune when you've got the bucks. Money can solve all your problems.

The other powerful and subtle deception that drives people today is the "you can get rich quick" mirage. People believe against all reasonable odds that they will be the next big winner. This is gold fever. I have talked with old miners in Colorado who tell stories of men who left their families, sold ranches and homes, worked themselves to death being driven by this disease. Few cash in. We used to have to travel to Las Vegas or Reno to witness this compulsion. But today we see the lie working its magic in the state lotteries and national sweepstakes. The time and energy and money American men and women devote to this obsession is absolutely astounding.

B. F. Skinner did behavior-modification experiments with chickens. He found that he could teach a chicken to peck at a disk if he rewarded the bird with a piece of corn. If he stopped rewarding the chicken, the chicken would quit pecking the disk. But if he gave an intermittent reward, that is, dropped a piece of corn only occasionally and at random, chickens would stand and peck relentlessly at the disk until they fell over from exhaustion. This is the psychological principle behind the compelling power of the slot machine.

We are driven and manipulated by the intermittent reward principle in sweepstakes, lotteries and gambling. Sure, sometimes people do get rich quick. If it never happened, we would soon give up the obsession. I read last week of a man in Colorado who won two $10,000 prizes in the lottery in one week. That ought to keep Coloradans pecking the lottery disk for months. But it's not just sweepstakes and gambling that are empowered by the principle of the slot-machine-type reward.

Even legitimate business dealings and the stock market can become a driving force with men who are susceptible to the mirage and the intermittent reward principle.

People are deceived by this mental contest. It is a kind of sleight-of-hand trick—our eyes are always on the big winner. We don't see the millions who are led astray by the get-rich-quick schemes. We somehow block out the reality of countless lives that are ruined by this obsession. We don't see the millions of elderly people who, duped by the sweepstakes and lottery myths, are pouring their Social Security checks into these things and then going without food and other necessities. And we do not stop long enough to think about the fact that even if we do become wealthy it is not in itself any assurance that we will truly be happy.

I started playing racquetball several years ago. I bought a ten-dollar racquet at K-mart, and I played in my old running shoes. But as I got a little better, I invested in an eighty-dollar racquet and eventually bought a pair of seventy-five-dollar shoes. I used to throw my K-mart racquet and old shoes on top of the locker when I went to take a shower. I never locked my car to protect my gym bag. There was nothing in it worth worrying about. But now that I have more expensive equipment, I always lock my car. I never leave the racquet and shoes on top of the locker. I spend a lot of time thinking about protecting the valuable things I have.

Money is like this. The more you have, the more management it requires. There are tremendous stresses in the investment area, in making secure our material possessions, in worrying about whether we are taking the right advice, making the right choices. During the stock market crash late in 1987, a man went to his broker's with a gun. He killed several men and women in that office before killing himself. For the person under the spell of money, the only thing worse than not having it is to have it and lose it.

Money: The Emotional Side

My personal struggle with money issues is on the emotional side. I do not feel driven to have things. It is fairly easy for me to keep a car for years and be satisfied with it, running the mileage up to over 150,000. But it is harder for me to stand by and watch certain members of my family get a lot of attention just because they have money. It is hard to attend family gatherings when everybody is talking money and I don't have anything to talk about. At times it has seemed like there is only one language that makes sense to my family, and I don't know the language.

Maybe you can relate. Money has always been important in my family. Living according to Christian values has meant very little to most of my family. Recently things have begun to change, but for most of my life it was money and the things money could do and buy that turned everybody on.

My older brother has been in business. He is good at making money. When he is going strong, he attracts the rest of the family to him like bees to honey. This has been hard for me. I have been tempted to get into investment schemes and to spend more time than I should thinking about and managing money because I want deep down to be accepted by my family. I want the attention that having money seems to bring.

Just as sex is never just sex, money is never just money. It is almost always something else. Something deeper is going on in us than the pure motivation to make money. One powerful motivating factor is that having money feeds feelings of self-worth. You always hear people say things like "He's worth two million." This is how who we are gets mixed up with how much money we have. If you have made a lot of money, it becomes easier to think of yourself as a hard worker, bright, diligent, clever and even superior to all those who have tried and failed. Having money can make us feel good about ourselves. We can also understand by thinking this through why people go crazy when they lose money. If their feelings of self-worth are tied to their portfolio, then a significant loss in the stock market is really a significant loss of self-esteem. Once you were somebody. Now you are nobody. For many it is too much to take.

The emotional need for security also fuels this obsession with money. Having money, things, insurance, a well-endowed retirement account make us feel that we are in control of our lives. This is a great battle Christians have to fight. Our central act of obedience is to give our lives to God in Christ, to relinquish control of our lives. Our temptation here is to say we trust God with our lives, but to retain personal control with a high degree of financial padding. It is this sin that Jesus addresses in the parable of the rich fool in Luke 12:16-21.

In the parable a rich man produces a good crop too big to store in his present barns. He decides to tear down his buildings and build bigger ones to store his grain and his goods. He says to himself: "You have plenty of good things laid up for many years. Take life easy; eat, drink and be merry." But God says to the rich man: "You fool! This very night your life will be demanded from you. Then who will get what you have prepared for yourself?" Jesus tells his followers, "This is how it will be with anyone who stores up things for himself but is not rich toward God."

The parable puts things in perspective. We think money can give us the security we desire, but it can't. True security can only be found in God. We need to pursue with our lives God and God's work, not money. This may be the hardest area for us. What we want to develop is a childlike faith and a deep trust that our father in heaven will provide for us in this life and the life to come. Without this kind of trust we will never be free. Our faith is built in this area as we give up personal control and put more of our lives into God's hands. Then we begin to see how he really will bless us as he has promised in Matthew 6:25-34.

Think of how your own children trust you as father to provide their meals, their clothing, the things they need. They don't feel like they have to take leftover food and pack it into their dresser drawers or stockpile hand-me-down clothing for some future date. They believe in you. You have always provided what they need. They believe you will continue to provide for their basic needs. This is faith. If only we as adults could do as well in our relationship with our father in heaven.

Try God in this area. Trust him. Give up your desire to stockpile. See if your father in heaven isn't up to the task of meeting your family's every authentic need.

Money: A Theological Perspective

Our misuse of money is rooted in a perversion of our call to dominion. In the beginning God created everything that exists; then he created man and woman. He said, "Let us make man in our image, in our likeness, and let them rule over the fish of the seas and the birds of the air, over the livestock, over all the earth, and over all the creatures that move along the ground" (Gen 1:26). We have been made stewards over God's varied resources. We have the responsibility to rightly manage those things that are in our lives by the grace of our loving God. But we do not have rights to those things. This is where we go wrong with money and things. We want the gift, but forget the giver. We live for money and the things of the earth rather than living our lives for God.

There are three biblical concepts that can help us to keep clear on this issue. The first is that God made everything. He created everything there is out of love for us and to provide for our needs on the earth. A Deuteronomy passage talking about God's people entering the promised land captures and beautifully describes this truth. God tells the writer he will give his people "a land with large, flourishing cities you did not build, houses filled with all kinds of good things you did not provide, wells you did not dig, and vineyards and olive groves you did not plant—then when you eat and are satisfied, be careful that you do not forget the Lord, who brought you out of Egypt, out of the land of slavery" (Deut 6:10-12).

The truth is, every good thing comes down from the Father above (Jas 1:17). The temptation is to forget this, to forget him, to indulge ourselves without thanksgiving and to see ourselves as owning the land, wells, vineyards and olive groves. If we own them, we can do with them as we please. If they are ours, we can spend them on our lusts. This perversion contributes to our greed. This is the effect of the Fall on our call to dominion.

One practical problem with remembering who owns the earth and everything in it comes from the fact that we do live today in a largely manmade environment. Just about everything we touch in our everyday lives, this keyboard, these clothes, the money we handle, cars, tools, everything around us, is crafted by human hands. What we haven't made, we've purchased. We bought the land; we dug the well; we planted the vineyards and olive trees. They belong to us. It's easy to slip into this way of thinking. So we have to remind ourselves often that everything that is here is here because of our loving Creator God.

This leads to our second main point. God retains ownership of everything he created. God says the whole earth is his (Ex 19:5-6 and Job 41:11). God says: "I have no need of a bull from your stall or of goats from your pens, for every animal of the forest is mine, and the cattle on a thousand hills. I know every bird in the mountains, and the creatures of the field are mine. If I were hungry I would not tell you, for the world is mine, and all that is in it" (Ps 50:8-12).

The third important point has already been mentioned. Christians are stewards of God's creation. He gives us responsibility to manage properly those gifts of the earth he has created for our provision and the provision of others. As stewards, our primary responsibility is to guide the use of God's resources, distributing God's blessings according to his divine purposes. This is truly a humble work we undertake as Christians. To do it right requires wisdom from above and guidance from the Holy Spirit of God.

The danger in the concept of stewardship dominion is that we can misunderstand the nature of the call and in a perverted way see it as a call to a high position. We can falsely assume that our stewardship of God's resources as Christians positions us above others. We can act sinfully as stewards by making others dependent upon us or by secretly enjoying the power involved in distributing God's goods according to our wishes. Instead, this call should be most humbling to us. If there is any crown in this, it is a crown of thorns. A line from Jacques Ellul's *Money and Power* puts Christian stewardship in its proper perspective. Of the sin of feeling superior or dominating others by controlling God's resources, the writer says, "It forgets that God's possessions belong to Christ, and in him to our neighbor, the one who is deprived of what we own."[1]

You and God's Money

The question "What shall I do with my money?" is really very similar to the question "What shall I do with my life?" The true nature of things is that if I belong to God, everything I have belongs to God. This means my life is not my own, but God's. It also means my money is not my own, but God's. The real question then becomes "What shall I do with God's money?" W. A. Smart has said:

We think of "giving God his part," a tithe or some other amount, and then keeping the rest as "our part" to be used without further responsibility to God. When we have paid God his tenth we are satisfied and God should be, for he has had what is his. We do not come in sight of Jesus and his thinking until we realize that we cannot give God anything but our love, and certainly we cannot buy from him the right to use nine-tenths of our money for purposes aside from his interests. The challenge of money is not to my purse but to my soul, and what we need is not the mathematics of giving as much as regeneration.[2]

Most of the teaching of Jesus about money is aimed not at the poor who are without it, but at those who have money and need to get rid of it, who have made money and the pursuit of money the central focus of their lives. To live for money and for what money can do for us is to live for ourselves. This is antithetical to the call of the gospel. To live for Christ is to relinquish control of our lives and to daily seek to lay our lives (and our money) down for others. To live for money or things is to live primarily for ourselves, no matter how much or how little we may have. Our lives cannot go in both directions at the same time. Jesus made this clear when he said, "You cannot serve both God and Money" (Lk 16:13).

I will not enter here into the debate about which economic system incorporates to the greatest degree our Christian principles.[3] Not that this is an unimportant question or that the economic system within which we work does not relate to the way we make decisions regarding our Christian commitments in the financial area. Whether we believe capitalism or another system is best suited to meeting world economic needs certainly will impact our personal economic choices. But my concern in this small chapter is to center on matters of the heart and on the practical application of basic scriptural principles to our personal discipleship.

The key question for us is this: "How much of God's resources do I really need to live?" This is a lifestyle question. It should be a question we continually raise under the accountability of the Spirit and our brothers and sisters in Christ. It is a question that should be asked and viewed in the context of the economic situation of the whole world in which we live. Most of us are already extremely rich by the standards of the rest of the world. Keeping this awareness present in our minds can help guide us in making the tough choices we need to make. Our goal in this area is to work continually to reduce our lifestyle requirements so that we can live well below our means. This opens up great possibilities for us of following the Spirit's leading and putting increasingly greater portions of God's financial blessings to work in the world.

The Lost Art of Tithing

The concept of the tithe is diminishing in American church culture. Anyone who grew up in a conservative church environment in previous generations was taught to tithe. Many of the younger converts in our day have not even heard of the tithe. Churches have gotten away from teaching it. We have stopped talking about money because we have wanted to counteract the negative view that the church is more interested in money than people. But we have lost something by de-emphasizing the tithe. If there is no practical biblical guideline to help hold us accountable we have a hard time battling the power of our lust for money and things. Sin often wins out. If we don't think this through we'll soon be back to putting a dollar a week in the collection plate.

The tithe concept is rooted in the Old Testament record of Jacob's vow to return a tenth of the Lord's blessings to God's house (Gen 28:22). The concept is retained throughout the Old Testament and usually refers to giving the firstborn of flocks and a tenth of the harvest to festive meals and toward support of the priests and those in need (Deut 14:22-29).

In the New Testament the emphasis is away from the legal prescription of the tithe toward the larger issues of sacrificial giving. Jesus, for instance, renounced the Pharisees for their legalistic observance of the tithe while neglecting more significant matters of love and justice (Mt 23:23; Lk 11:42). For New Testament Christians the broader and more weighty matters of

personal sacrifice stretch the concept of the tithe. Jesus said we
are to sell all and turn away from our possessions (Mt 19:21).
The book of Acts testifies to the reality of this kind of deep
sacrifice occurring in the early Christian community when it
says: "No one claimed that any of his possessions was his own,
but they shared everything they had. . . . There were no needy
persons among them. For from time to time those who owned
lands or houses sold them, brought the money from the sales
and put it at the apostles' feet, and it was distributed to anyone
as he had need" (Acts 4:32-35).

The tithe as a starting place for Christian giving does not
even have to be argued biblically to make good sense. Think
of everything you have, every blessing, everything God has giv-
en you and done for you. What would be a proper portion of
your income and resources to return to the Lord out of grat-
itude for what he's done? When you start thinking like that, the
idea of returning a tenth to the Lord's work sounds stingy. God
has given us everything we need and many of the things we
want as well. He has been incredibly generous with us. How
can we, in the face of this kind of love and generosity, not be
moved to give sacrificially to see that God's work is not hin-
dered in the world?

In our men's Bible study the other morning we got onto the
topic of how our kids commonly respond when they are asked
to do some yardwork or housework. The normal thing is for
them to want to get paid. Here we are as parents feeding the
kids, clothing them, paying for their sports activities and equipment, their school activities and books and supplies, their
entertainments. We pay doctor bills, we provide housing,
we buy cars, we keep them filled with gas, we chauffeur the
kids around, and on top of all this we even give them allow-
ances. Then one day we ask them to mow the lawn or paint the
fence. They look us in the eye and ask, "Uh, are we getting
paid?"

Later on, as I thought about our discussion, I realized that as adults we often view and treat our Father in heaven in a similar way. One hundred per cent of all our needs, physical and spiritual, are covered by God. He pours out his blessings upon us without reserve. Then he says, "Keep what you need to raise your family and even enjoy many of the luxuries of life. But do not forget me or my work on the earth." What is our common response? We even flinch at the entry-level commitment. Ten per cent! Isn't that a little much, Lord? Couldn't you really do with less? I don't know if I can make it on ninety per cent.

I know money is a sensitive topic. And I'm not trying to lay a guilt trip on you. Judie and I have been all over the map on this issue. We started our giving in the Catholic church many years ago. There we put a dollar each week in the collection plate, and thought we were being generous with what we had. Later we began attending a conservative, Bible-teaching church where we were taught about tithing. There it was a legalistic thing. The Holy Spirit was seen as having little to do with our giving. But we started tithing—ten per cent came off the top. It was a struggle at first, but we eventually managed it. Things were going well. We adopted twins and moved into our first house in the same year. Judie and I were both able to keep working. But within a few months a surprise element entered in. We found out that Judie was pregnant. When Gabe arrived we had three babies. Judie could no longer work outside the home. Our income was suddenly and drastically cut in half. Within a year we were forced to go on a county social services program to get free milk and eggs. We still gave a portion of our income to the church, but we could not make the tithe without becoming more dependent on government programs. We know how hard this can be.

If things are tough for you right now, the Lord knows. He loves you. If you have lost your job and you're in transition, don't carry an extra burden of guilt about maintaining a tithe. Or you may be a single parent now trying to make it on one income. Recognize the fact that your giving patterns will have to change for a time while you go through transition and try to find your balance again. God's grace is active in the extraordinary situations of our lives. On the other hand, you might be surprised at how much you can still give to the Lord during tough times if you are willing to do the difficult but needed work of budgeting your money, watching your spending, and setting goals for giving to God. The goal should always be to build back up to a tithe as the Lord blesses you, and further, to think creatively about how you can go beyond the tithe to deeper sacrificial giving.

The tithe should be retained in the teaching of the Christian church. It is a practical guide for giving today. It helps us to be accountable to God in the area of our finances. But the tithe should be seen as a starting point, otherwise we are tempted to return to the legalism of the Pharisees. It is easy to think that once we have made a tithe we have completed our obligation toward God and his work. For Christians the challenge is much greater. It is to continually think of new ways to increasingly give more of the resources God brings into our lives to further accomplish his purposes in the world.

Some of you can give far more than ten per cent. For you, giving ten per cent is no more sacrificial than tossing a dollar in the plate would be for others. You can set your sights much higher. Think creatively and plan intentionally for deeper sacrificial giving. If you are already living at a comfortable level and you've made appropriate financial choices regarding the education of your children, your retirement and reasonable insurance for the family, consider giving all future salary increases to the Lord's work. Imagine how much could be accomplished with this single act of obedience.

And if you're saving for retirement, how much do you really

need? Calculate it to the best of your ability. Once you have what you think will be enough, why save more? Why continue building bigger and bigger barns? Drive a stake for the Lord at this point and for the rest of your life give all the money that used to go to your retirement program to the Lord's work instead.

One friend tithes his money and his property. Of the total number of apartments he owns, he dedicates one out of every ten to the Lord to provide free housing to individuals and families in need. I know of doctors, dentists, psychiatrists and lawyers who tithe a portion of their professional time to seeing and treating those who do not have the ability to pay. I have heard of numerous innovative plans developed by creative Christian men for deepening Christian giving. The great Christian leader and businessman R. G. LeTourneau lived on ten per cent of his income and gave ninety per cent away.

Those of you whom God has richly blessed ought to get together with your peers and brainstorm ways to put your extra wealth to work for the Lord. Jesus said, "For everyone who has been given much, much will be demanded; and from the one who has been entrusted with much, much more will be asked" (Lk 12:48). Form accountable relationships with your friends and make creative choices that will put your money to work for God.

I heard a story of a wealthy man who went to visit his pastor because he was troubled by the concept of the tithe. He told the pastor that he had made over half a million dollars that year in real estate. He explained that if he were to tithe his income it would mean that he would have to give fifty thousand dollars to the church. The pastor was sympathetic. He told the man he understood the difficulty of his position. He asked if they could pray together and both men lowered their heads. The pastor then prayed simply, "Lord, please reduce this man's income until he can afford to tithe."

Gaining Power over Money

There are a number of things we can do that will help us take control of our lust for money and things. Here are just a few ideas that can prove beneficial.

Stay close to the Bible and its teachings on money. Reading and rereading the biblical material, especially the teachings of Jesus on money, will help us to maintain a proper perspective in this area. Jesus says, "Sell your possessions and give to the poor" (Lk 12:33). He says, "Give to anyone who asks you, and if anyone takes what belongs to you, do not demand it back" (Lk 6:30). If our hearts are open to the Spirit of God, we cannot read and think on passages like these without being changed. Do everything you can to expose yourself to the biblical teachings on money and its proper place in the kingdom of God.

Find ways to keep in touch with the poor. We can spend too much time with people who have money. Then it is easy to lose perspective and get out of touch with reality.

Our family sat in a restaurant in Vail, Colorado, and listened to two teen-age girls talk. The one girl complained nonstop for fifteen minutes about how poor her family was. She told her friend that the family across the road from them had three swimming pools, and her family had only one. The other family had over a dozen horses, and she had only three. The other family went to Hawaii for three months every winter. Her family had to vacation in Florida and California.

I remember the looks of astonishment on my own kids' faces as they listened in on the conversation at the next table. We compare ourselves with our wealthy neighbors, and we think we're poor. We think we're poor because we drive a new Ford rather than a Mercedes. We think we're poor because we have an old microwave oven that sets the time manually with dials instead of one with pushbutton, computer-regulated programming. We have to work at reminding ourselves how rich we really are. We need a regular dose of reality to keep us on track.

Judie and I just spent two weeks with our family on a short-term work trip to Lily of the Valley Home for Girls in San Lucas, Guatemala. One Sunday afternoon I had the privilege of visiting with a couple of friends at three churches in zone 21, one of the poorest sections in Guatemala City. The third church we visited was in an area where there was no electricity. The church was a simple block building with a dirt floor. A single kerosene lantern burned near the front and cast a flickering light on the faded pink and white crepe-paper decorations. I was surprised when the pastor turned and without notice invited me to bring the message for the day. He told the congregation that God has a purpose for everything. He thought we as visitors must have a word from God for the congregation. Perhaps we did. I did preach. But I believe God's purpose behind our visit was more for those of us who were visiting. After I preached, the congregation took up a love offering for me as a visiting preacher. Out of the little they had they gave generously to me. It was a humbling lesson I will never forget.

My children, too, had a similar experience. One of the young women who worked at the home had a friend with a unique ministry in Guatemala City. She asked our teen-agers if they would like to go along and visit her friend. They decided to go.

They were surprised when Sue drove them to the city trash dump. There they saw that people had set up shanties on the heaps of refuse. They lived in the dump, ate food from the dump, used cardboard and other materials from the trash to build their huts. They visited with Kari, the twenty-six-year-old American woman who rents a building next to the dump. There she has created a school and a refuge. She teaches seventy kids from the dump and feeds them two good meals each day. She is supported by American friends. She told our kids stories of how garbage trucks would sometimes back in and dump trash on small children without seeing them. Those children would often suffocate and die under the pile of rubble.

It was a life-changing experience for our young people. Everything they see now is played against the image they hold in their minds of the people living at the dump in Guatemala City. They will never again see an American supermarket or a toy store or commercials on TV in the same way.

Stay in touch with the world's poor. Stay in touch with the poor in your own community. You will have a better chance of keeping a realistic perspective on money and things if you do.

Pray about money and how to use it. It is in prayer that we can confess our greed and be led by the Spirit to make appropriate changes in our lifestyle and our use of God's resources. It is in prayer that we can hear God speak to us about our feelings and attitudes toward money. He can help us understand why we cling to money when we do. He can help us to understand our history and how our parents and others have contributed to our attitudes and dispositions toward money and things. God will speak to us in prayer and guide us toward greater freedom from the bondage and power wealth and possessions can exert over our lives. And pray about your giving. It is only right to ask God how much you should give and where you can best put his money to work.

Form accountable relationships. Most of us still view money as a private affair. We don't like to think of others meddling in our finances. But like other obsessions we may have, money cannot be adequately dealt with if it remains a private matter. We are too prone to rationalization. A good place to start is by studying and discussing family financial matters with your wife. Discuss how the biblical principles you study together can be lived out more effectively. If you are not married, a good friend with a similar interest will be a help to you. The intention is that you face regularly the issue of money. Choose to be accountable to someone in this area.

Judie and I have always had an outside financial counselor. We have found it tremendously helpful to lay out our finances to a third person who is good with money and also a committed Christian. It is hard to admit your weaknesses to another person. But it is difficult and perhaps impossible to grow beyond your present level without this vulnerability. Do you want to gain control over your finances and serve God more effectively? If you do, then seek the help and accountability an honest relationship with a Christian brother or sister can bring.

Develop a countercultural attitude toward money. Our culture idolizes money. Men and women who have uncritically accepted the cultural view will expect you to believe certain things and act in certain ways with regard to money. Gaining a Christian mind toward money will make you counterculture. It will help you to keep your head when the pressure is on.

I remember getting a call from a friend one night. She started the conversation with "How would you and Judie like to double your income in the next year and become financially free within five years?" I answered her honestly by saying, "That really wouldn't interest us at all." There was silence on the other end. I went on to talk about many of the things mentioned in this chapter. Life is more than making money. Making money does not make you free. The things in my life that I would have to give up in order to spend more time making money would be too big a sacrifice to make. Once you get into the money game, it is hard to find a place where you can stop, where you decide you've had enough. No, we wouldn't be interested.

The reason the phone went dead on the other end is that the question she asked is designed as a hook that cannot fail. The culture expects you to be interested in making money, the more the better. Everyone is supposed to answer yes to that no-fail question which then leads into a discussion of the program or scheme that is supposed to deliver on the promise. Those who sell their get-rich-quick schemes have no comeback if you're not interested in getting rich quick. Developing a countercultural attitude can help you to stay out of things that will swallow up your valuable time.

Another countercultural action that will strengthen you and help you gain control over money is to give your money away. Nothing breaks the bondage money may have over you more than this. In giving it we are stating with our actions that money is not the most important thing in our lives. If you struggle and go through agony just thinking about parting with some of your hard-earned cash, then you need to start giving it away. You might even need to begin by giving it in ways that seem foolish. Give it to kids who come to your door selling things. Give it to them, and then don't take the thing they are selling. Give money to people you don't even know. If you run into people who have hit hard times, give them some money. And, of course, don't forget to be giving regularly in the important traditional ways as well, to your church and to other Christian endeavors God places on your heart. I have always felt that ten per cent should go to your home church first, and you should be looking for places beyond that to give more and give it freely. The goal is to get to the place where you actually enjoy giving it away. Then you are free indeed.

Another cultural phenomenon related to money is the favoritism shown to people who have it. Our countercultural reaction will be to refuse to show this kind of favoritism. Whether someone has money or not should never determine how we treat that person (Jas 2:1-13). This is another way we refuse to be controlled by money. This is an important way that we rise above the cultural idolization of mammon.

A related idea is to work to demonstrate by your decisions and actions that you prize people above money. Too often people are used as a means to the selfish end of gaining more money. If we refuse to see people in this way and refuse to use them for our profit, we will take another step toward gaining control over money. We will be denying the power of money to diminish our values and depersonalize our relationships.

Money can destroy marriages, friendships, families, business relationships. If we are countercultural, we will never let money come between us and those we love and those for whom Christ died. The money problems that come up in a relationship will never have the power to control us on the personal level. If we have no lust for money, we can lose money and forget about it, putting it out of our minds, or even be cheated and still find that we are able to forgive. But if we love money and lose it, or love money and get cheated out of it, it will eat at us and embitter us. We can pray that God will set us free from our love for money.

Develop the basic skills for money management. Some simple budgeting and goal setting in the financial area can eliminate a great deal of frustration and tension. Learn to do a budget that reflects your personal and biblical goals for what you want to accomplish with the money that comes into your life. Measure where your money is going.

A good check on whether you are accomplishing what you intend is to see whether your checkbook shows that you are commonly spending money in the places and in the percentages that are desirable according to your goals. Keep track for a month of your loose change spending. You may be surprised at how much of your monthly income is depleted by impulse buying of frivolous, useless or unhealthy commodities. You have to know where your money is being spent if you are ever going to make a reasonable attempt to bring intentionality into your spending.

Learn as much as you can about good financial planning so that you can make the most of the money God brings into your life. This is what it means to be a good steward. Burying our money is not the best thing to do. We can make more intelligent choices with the money we have so that we can do even more with it for the good of others. There is excellent financial counseling available in many churches today and in the private sector with competent Christian financial people. Make use of these resources to learn and grow in this area. It is important to receive financial help from Christians who share the same values and purposes you do regarding stewardship of the resources of God.

Work to develop attitudes that guard you in the financial area. One important attitudinal reality is the way we view advertising. Advertising drives our love of money and our sense of need for material things. Advertising has only two messages. The first is that you do not yet have all the things you need to be happy. The second is that the things you already have are not good enough. We have to get control of this. We have to learn to be satisfied with less and to enjoy living on less if we are ever going to be truly happy. We have to make a conscious effort to do mental battle against the powerful advertisements which are incredibly successful in persuading, motivating and manipulating us into acting contrary to what we know is biblically right about our use of money.

Another place where our attitudes can be shaped is in the area of impulse buying. Going shopping is the great American pastime. There is nothing wrong with shopping if we have decided that a certain purchase is a necessity and we are out comparing prices and the quality of different makes and models. But to just go shopping opens us to endless possibilities for frivolous spending. Sitting at home looking through the catalogs is no better. Something is always catching our eye. The new television buying shows capitalize on this great American obsession. Most of the time we do not really need the thing we purchase on impulse. We should choose our shopping in the same way that we choose our television programming. We should look at the choices available and decide to tune in programs that will be particularly good. Instead the pattern is usually to just turn on the TV and then sit in front of it all evening. We should never just watch TV; we should watch programs. We should not just go shopping; we should shop for particular things that we have already determined through careful consideration and prayer that we really need.

Develop a deep hatred for the incredible pressure put on us to charge things when we do not have the money to buy them. We are constantly tempted by easy terms that are not really easy at all, and the trick of no payments until January. We have this incredible ability to convince ourselves that we will somehow be better off in January than we are now. This is not a rational belief for people who know they are living in a fallen world. Throw away the credit card offers you get in the mail without even opening them up. Cut up the cards you already have. Get tough on credit buying. If you can't seem to get out of the hole, get help. Get counseling on your finances and form the accountable relationships we have talked about before. This may be the area most prone to obsession in our day. Credit is so easy, and the desire to have prestige and the power of money so strong that when these things meet in us, there is great potential for destruction.

Emphasize quality rather than quantity in your lifestyle. Don't accept the world's lie that the meaning of life is in the number of things you possess. Remind yourself daily that who you are is not determined by what you have but by who you know. Knowing Christ brings a sense of value to your soul that having things can never achieve. And following his call to reach the world in his name gives meaning to your life that money cannot buy. Having this attitude will keep you on the right road.

Christian Wealth and Biblical Priorities

There are several biblical priorities that can guide us in what to do with the resources God brings into our life. First, Christians are in communion with the world's poor and the suffering and life problems of those in need. The Greek root for the biblical word *communion* means "to share." Our highest priority should be to share what we have in every way we can to bring support and help to those who are currently in need. I say currently in need because economic and personal need is a shifting reality. We will sometimes be in a position to give. At other times we will be on the receiving end. Paul writes in 2 Corinthians 8:13-15: "Our desire is not that others might be relieved while you are hard pressed, but that there might be equality. At the present time your plenty will supply what they need, so that in turn their plenty will supply what you need. Then there will be equality, as it is written: 'He who gathered much did not have too much, and he who gathered little did not have too little.' "

If we gather much, if our resources are great, our biblical obligation is to share out of our abundance with those who have less. We will remember the rich fool chastised for building bigger and bigger barns (Lk 12:13-21). We are not given wealth to lavish it on ourselves, but to share it in the world. Christians should be known for their generosity. Christians should be known for their chosen solidarity with the world's poor, having a lifestyle that demonstrates a desire to be in communion with the elements of need and suffering in the world. To share. That is our number-one priority for life. That is the mark of our Christian love.

The second priority is to deny the world. Christians can choose simplicity and live reasonably and responsibly in a world that has gone crazy with consumerism and greed. By denying the world's powerful promotion of money as the meaning of life, we stand as models of another way, a better way, to live a life free from the obsession with money and things. If there is no observable way to distinguish us from our culture, then we are not doing well as Christians in the area of lifestyle.

A simpler lifestyle may include a smaller house and less luxurious furnishings, fewer cars and older cars and the choice of public transportation. Simplicity may include deciding to get out of the time-gobbling, high-pressure occupations that rob us of opportunities to minister love and care in our families and neighborhoods and to serve Christ fully with our gifts. By denying the dominant lifestyle of our culture we can lift and model quality life at its best. Consumerism is not the meaning of life and can never be ultimately fulfilling. Christ can. Christian simplicity will not only model a different way of living, it will help us as Christians to be happier, healthier, more excited about the truly significant things in life and increasingly better able to live on less and enjoy it more.

The final thing I will mention in the area of wealth is that those of us who have wealth ought to make it a priority to speak for those who do not. The toughest question for us to face is whether we really represent God and live according to his priorities in the world. As proof to John the Baptist that he was the Messiah, Jesus said, "Go back and report to John what you hear and see: The blind receive sight, the lame walk, those who have leprosy are cured, the deaf hear, the dead are raised, and the good news is preached to the poor" (Mt 11:4-5). Could we give a similar measure of the fruit of our lives and ministry as proof that we belong to God? Do we have a deep concern for the blind, the lame, the deaf, the poor? Do we raise in our public circles the cause of those who have no voice or status of their own? Perhaps we have to confess that we do not really share Jesus' love and concern for the poor and oppressed.

One theologian remarks:

Why do atheistic systems like Marxism prosper among the oppressed far more than Christianity? Is it because the poor have known only a church captive to its culture, or even worse, one lending its justification to a system that perpetuates gross injustices and inequalities? Where is the prophetic voice of Jesus in the church that says with courage and integrity, "Blessed are you poor" and "Woe to you rich." Are we all too silent because we have lost so much of our integrity, or because we do not want to prophesy against ourselves.[4]

The temptation will be to ignore the poor. It has been so from the early days of the church (Jas 2:1-13). We have to ask ourselves why so many American churches have no ministry to the poor and few members who are poor. The church should be filled with those who are in need. The gospel is the good news to the poor. Are we preaching this gospel from our pulpits and through our individual lives?

What is your temptation in the area of money and wealth? Does greed have too much power in your life? Do you feel peer pressure or family pressure to be somebody and making money seems like the only way to prove yourself? Do you need to get out of debt to be free? Do you need to change your lifestyle to be free? Is it important to you to be obedient in this area?

I can't help but think again of that twenty-six-year-old American woman who built a school for the Lord in the garbage dump in Guatemala City. How did she break away from the American dream to do something significant for the poor? What kinds of lifestyle choices did she have to make to extend love, food and the hope of education to the poor of Guatemala in Christ's name? What material things does she go without so that those who have nothing have a chance at something? Was it easier for her than it would be for you and me?

What will you do?

Questions for Groups and Individuals

1. The author contends that money does not free us, but drives us. (p. 137) Can you give a personal illustration of the truth of this?

2. The author discussed various ways that money may grab us emotionally. (p. 141) Do you agree or disagree with his assessment of the effect money can have on us? Why?

3. How can good theology help release us from the hold money has over us?

4. The author says that the key question we should ask ourselves when we make decisions related to money is, "How much of God's resources do I really need to live?" (p. 146) If you asked yourself this question seriously right now, what is one practical difference it might make in how you spend, invest or give away your money?

5. Of the various suggestions offered in the section on gaining power over money (pp. 152-59) which ones do you already practice? What is one strategy you think you will include in your life after reading this?

What are some of the suggestions you particularly resist? Why do you think you resist them?

6. Does the lifestyle of Christian simplicity described at the end of the chapter appeal to you? If so, what obstacles do you see standing in the way of your practicing such a lifestyle? What is one practical way you could move toward a lifestyle of greater simplicity?

7/THE TEMPTATION TO BE PERFECT

The desires of men are insatiable.
In Eden, there emerged a desire to become perfect
and establish equality with God.
JEREMY BENTHAM

Anything that's really worth doing is worth doing badly.
G. K. CHESTERTON

*T*he desire for the perfect in this life is a sin.

Bob Oerter, pastor for many years of First Presbyterian Church in Boulder, Colorado, told a story one Sunday morning about how he was taken aside as a young man by an older pastor who told him that what he really needed was a second blessing of God that would make him perfect. Bob listened politely for some time as the older man described in detail the experience that had blessed him with spiritual perfection some fourteen years earlier. He told Bob that he had not sinned against God or man since that decisive event. Bob said he glanced up then to the older man's wife who was standing silently behind her husband. She looked weary and disinterested. When Bob caught her eye, she just shook her head, rolled her eyes, and waved her hand at her husband's back in such a way as to say, "Don't believe a word of it."

Absolute perfection is a quality found only in God. Adam and Eve were perfect man and perfect woman because they were created exactly the way God wanted to create them. But Adam and Eve were not satisfied to be perfect man and woman. They wanted the greater perfection. They wanted equality with God.

Anytime you and I desire, expect or claim to achieve Godlike perfection in this life we are playing with fire. Our claim is blasphemous. We are saying that we believe we can attain the perfection of God through right thinking and action. If this were true, we would no longer need a Savior. We could save ourselves.

I remember hearing once that Moroccans deliberately weave errors into their fine rugs. They believe the attempt to be perfect is blasphemous. The errors woven into the patterns of their rugs are there to remind them that humans are only human, and only God is God.

If the desire to be perfect is a sin, then what are we living for? What is a proper goal for human life and work? How are we to understand Jesus when he says, "Be perfect, therefore, as your heavenly Father is perfect?" (Mt 5:48).

The Greek root of this word *perfect* is *telos,* which expresses the idea of reaching our appointed end or purpose. In the common Greek of the day the concept conveyed with this word was to become mature, an adult or fully grown. A complete study of the uses of the word *perfect* in the New Testament will convince you that the goal of perfection toward which we grow in the Christian life is maturity in Christ, a wholeness of mind and spirit that prepares us to meet life's demands with the resources of God.

This passage in Matthew has to be read and understood in its proper context. Jesus is talking about the constant and un-wavering kindness and love of the heavenly Father. It is this quality of unselfish love that should be found in us, God's children. This is the quality we are to emulate, the quality that will set us apart as mature believers. The perfection Jesus requires in his disciples is to grow up to be mature lovers in a world hungering for the love of Christ.

J. I. Packer writes: "No doubt when the Christian is perfected in glory he will be sinless, but to equate the biblical idea of perfection with sinlessness and then to argue that, because the Bible calls some men perfect, therefore sinlessness on earth must be a practical possibility, would be to darken counsel. The present perfection which, according to Scripture, some Christians attain is a matter, not of sinlessness, but of strong faith, joyful patience, and overflowing love."[1] The Bible nowhere equates the concept of perfection with sinlessness. The goal for us as Christians is to become complete and mature men through the power and grace of God in Christ. It is to develop mature Christian character which expresses itself in practical, Christlike love toward the world.

Anatomy of a Perfectionist

We are not all driven by perfectionism. Most of us do not really believe it is possible to live perfectly in this life. But most of us do have perfectionistic tendencies in some area that can create pressures and problems for us and rob us of our joy.

One husband joked with me about his wife who he claimed was an incredible perfectionist and neat freak in the house. He said he would often get up during the night to go to the bathroom and come back to find his side of the bed made. He claimed she was the only woman he knew who was so compulsive about messes that she put newspapers under the cuckoo clock.

Think about some of the following characteristics of perfectionistic people to see if any of them are true of you:

Do you expect the absolute best of yourself at all times?

Do you sometimes put off beginning an important project because you do not have the time to do it perfectly?

Do you get upset when things don't go the way you think they should go?

Do you find yourself getting upset with other people because they can't seem to understand your desire to get things done right?

Are you hard on yourself when you make a mistake?

Are you doubly hard on yourself when you make the same mistake twice?

Are you disappointed in others because of the lack of quality in their work?

Is the idea of being average in something distasteful to you?

Do you often think on finishing something that you could have done better?

If some of these hit home, you will want to read on.

Perfectionists tend to respond to life issues is similar ways. Dr. David Stoop, who wrote *Living with a Perfectionist,*[2] and David D. Burns, author of "The Perfectionist's Script for Self-Defeat,"[3] develop some key characteristics they claim can be found in most perfectionists.

Perfectionists tend to think in dichotomous categories. Everything in life is an either/or proposition. Either I am perfect or I am worthless. I am either a "great" father or I am a "bad" father. If I can't be the best writer, I am not going to write at all. If I am not always kind or unselfish or loving, then I am a worthless person.

Perfectionists engage in minimizing and maximizing. They tend to maximize failures and minimize successes. You might say to your perfectionistic wife, "That was a lovely dinner tonight, dear." She would reply in discouragement: "Oh, no. It was a horrible failure. The lemon was too tart in the meringue pie. I was so embarrassed. I'll never be able to have them back."

There is this common inability to accept all that went right because the all-consuming focus is on the small thing that went wrong. People who cannot accept a compliment usually suffer from this mental tangle.

This tendency is seen as well in the insurance salesman who has had the best year in his history with the company but is still depressed because he is not the top salesman in his division. It is seen in the young bank executive who stays late every night at work because he is afraid that if he doesn't stay late tonight he might be fired. It is seen in the man who cannot enjoy the fact that he has landed the new job because he felt he could have done better on several of the questions asked during the interview.

Perfectionists set unrealistic goals for themselves and others. The world of the perfectionist is an "as it *should* be" world. The ideal world that lives in the mind of the perfectionist is the background out of which goals and expectations are formed. Since the expectations are mental realities unattainable in the real world, the perfectionist is continually set up for failure. For the perfectionist, average is the same as mediocre, and even when something is well done, it could always have been done just a little bit better.

One of the areas in which I am personally perfectionistic is in my woodworking. I like to work with my hands, building furniture or making changes in the house. It has been difficult for me to enjoy the pieces I have finished because I find that my attention is always drawn toward the tiny, sometimes even nearly invisible, problem area on the piece. It always amazed me that others could look at something I made and not see the chip on the table leg I had to fill with wood putty or the joint that was not exact. Things that drove me crazy, Judie couldn't even see. She sometimes couldn't see them even after I pointed them out.

My area of growth here is to learn to be satisfied with my

good effort and to remember that the fruits of my labor do not have to be perfect to be enjoyed and used by my family. My shift in focus over the last several years has been to appreciate and enjoy more about the process of building and creating instead of focusing only on the perfection or lack of it in the final product.

If you are perfectionistic, you judge yourself by the quality of your achieved end. If it is flawed, you cannot feel good about it. You could not make the thing or the project or the relationship or whatever, come out in real life exactly as you had pictured it in your mind. The unrealistic goal robs us of our joy.

The other problem caused by unrealistic expectations is the pressure your perfectionistic standards place on all those around you. Your family, your friends, your neighbors, your coworkers will all fall short of what you think they ought to be. They will suffer because they can never fully please you. They will not be able to enjoy living or working with you. The unrealism of your perfectionism will make you a lonely man.

Perfectionists struggle with low self-esteem. If I measure my self-worth by my successful achievement, and my goals, standards and expectations are unrealistically high, there is no way I can ever feel good about myself. I have an all-or-nothing perspective on everything I attempt. I judge my worth by whether or not I have perfectly accomplished that which I set out to do. My goals are never met to my satisfaction. I feel empty, unsuccessful, worthless. So I set higher goals for next time and try even harder. But this is just more unrealism heaped on the unrealism of the past. It is a vicious cycle. Trying harder or creating even higher expectations only makes things worse. It is a miserable life.

A healthy perspective will allow you to objectively evaluate your performance and still feel good about yourself. When perfectionists evaluate their performance, they are really judging their personal worth.

Do Perfectionists Enjoy Greater Success?

David Burns describes perfectionists as "those whose standards are high beyond reach or reason, people who strain compulsively and unremittingly toward impossible goals and who measure their own worth entirely in terms of productivity and accomplishment." He concludes, "For these people, the drive to excel can only be self-defeating."[4]

Instead of greater success, perfectionists usually have decreased productivity over the long haul, health problems related to their type "A" behavior, frustration and often angry outbursts that show lack of self-control, difficulty in relationships and low self-image. Perfectionists commonly struggle with a number of emotional disorders including "depression, performance anxiety, test anxiety, social anxiety, writer's block, and obsessive-compulsive illness."[5]

In testing a group of sales people Burns discovered that those who were perfectionistic earned on the average $15,000 a year less than their peers who were not perfectionists. The perfectionist tends to take much more time than is practically possible to accomplish tasks at a greater degree of proficiency than is warranted. It is important to ask how good a thing needs to be in order to accomplish the desired end with a reasonable degree of quality and proficiency.

I remember that when I started teaching Bible classes, I would put in a tremendous amount of study and preparation time. I would use every available minute in preparation for the presentation I was going to make. After having more experience as a teacher, I began to see that the difference in practical response of people to the teaching I spent ten hours to develop was not significantly different than the practical response I observed toward another similar teaching assignment I had taken fifteen hours to prepare. If the extra five hours (fifty per cent more preparation time) makes practically no difference in the response of others to the work, then it is not worth doing when there are other important demands on my time. Certainly, if I have the time, I will benefit from five hours more of study and preparation. But I do not usually have that much extra time to spend, and it is healthier to accept a less than perfect product that is still good than it is to strive for perfection in one area and create time and priority problems in all the other important areas of my life.

Perfectionism appears to be counterproductive in athletics as well. Michael Mahoney did a study of top male gymnasts at Penn State and found that the elite group did not exhibit perfectionistic tendencies. As a whole they tended to "underemphasize the importance of past performance failures, while athletes who failed to qualify tended to rouse themselves to near panic states during competition through mental images of self-doubt and impending tragedy."[6] The performance anxiety of those who had perfectionistic tendencies kept them from excelling as gymnasts. Another study at Memphis State produced the same results with a group of racquetball players. Those with perfectionistic personalities had greater difficulty recovering from mistakes. Their perfectionism kept them from progressing in skill and attitude.

Another interesting study was conducted by Vice Dean Phyllis Beck at the Pennsylvania Law School. She looked closely at twenty-five law students who sought counseling shortly after entering the program. A majority of these students displayed a high degree of perfectionism. The school's admission standards are rigorous, and admission is very competitive. Students who apply are used to being at the top of the class at former schools. Now, lumped together as a group, these students had difficulty accepting the fact that they were no longer number one. When they see that their performance will place them somewhere in the middle of the pack, "they react with frustration, anger, depression, and panic. Because their previous experiences have left them psychologically unprepared for an 'average' role, they are prone to perceive themselves, unrealistically, as second-rate losers. Their self-respect plummets, and they experience a strong desire to withdraw from painful experiences."[7]

Perfectionism at the management level in business is now widely recognized as counterproductive to maintaining a creative atmosphere important for success in business. The perfectionists are too concerned with making every attempt come out right. Their demands for perfection inhibit the risk taking necessary for creative experimentation. In *In Search of Excellence,* Tom Peters writes, "A special attribute of the success-oriented, positive, and innovating environment is a substantial tolerance for failure." He goes on to quote a number of today's top business executives and includes a statement from Emerson's senior executive, Charles Knight, who says, "You need the ability to fail. You cannot innovate unless you are willing to accept mistakes." This is difficult to impossible for perfectionists. Their demands for perfection will make employees paranoid and afraid to fail. Employees will not risk failure when it inevitably leads to verbal abuse, angry outbursts or negative personnel evaluations. Perfectionism in management is counterproductive to achieving an atmosphere for creativity and innovation.[8]

Excellence and Perfectionism: What's the Difference?

David Stoop shows in his book that a fine line exists between the legitimate desire for excellence and the drive for the perfect that can enslave us. The pursuit of excellence will tend to work positively for a person if the desire is rooted in the real world of the possible. Perfectionism works against us because it is a striving for the ideal, the unreachable goal of the perfect in this imperfect world. The perfectionist really desires the impossible.

The language of the person whose goals are reasonable and realistic is usually characterized by such terms and phrases as "I would like" or "I hope to" or "I want to," stated in the

framework of a request or desire. The perfectionist is commonly heard to say, "I must" or "I should" or "I ought to," in a self-
deprecating or demanding manner.

The motivations are also different between a man seeking
excellence and the perfectionist. The first is hoping for the
positive, desiring success measured in realistic terms. The perfectionist, instead, is usually avoiding the negative, acting more
out of fear of failure, because his self-esteem is tied too closely
at the emotional level to his successful achievement.

A man desiring to grow in excellence will exhibit a healthy
response to experiences of failure. He will learn from his mistakes, accepting failure as common to human experience. But
the perfectionist will judge himself severely. He will say, "I must
never do that again—never. I should do better than that!" For
those who are perfectionistic, failure is unacceptable because
it is damaging to self-concept. The pursuit of excellence is a
challenge welcomed by the free man. But the perfectionist is
imprisoned and enslaved in an unrealism that makes every new
task a dreadful risk that threatens to be emotionally devastating.

The man pursuing excellence will be able to enjoy a sense
of accomplishment, success and fulfillment in life. The perfectionist instead will suffer continual frustration. To live for the
perfect leads to certain disappointment. When perfection is the
prerequisite for self-acceptance or the acceptance of others,
there will never be happiness with ourselves or those with
whom we work and live.

You would think that experience and the objective evidence
that nothing and no one in this world is perfect would convince
the perfectionist to give up his fantasy world. And, if the evidence didn't convince a person, you'd think the pure hell of
living in this emotional prison would.

The Price We Pay for Perfectionism
We've talked about the emotional problems caused by perfec-

tionism, touched on the relational difficulties and seen that perfectionists are not usually the most successful in their field. There are other major problems caused by perfectionism that are worth developing from a Christian perspective.

First, perfectionism harms and diminishes the relationship with God. The perfectionist acts out in his faith the belief that God wants his followers to be perfect as God is perfect. He drives himself to make up for past failures. He earnestly disciplines himself to live up to the standards set forth by his perfect God. But again, and again, and again he falls far short. This is a terrible trap. If God is really determining the quality of our relationship on the basis of how good we are or how much we accomplish, how do we ever know if we've done enough? There is always more we could do. This is tremendously guilt producing. If we think this way, we will grow to see God as punitive, aloof, demanding, uncaring. Some perfectionists wind up carrying anger toward God because he could have made a perfect world but didn't. Or they doubt the existence of God because they cannot see in the imperfect world the evidence for a perfect God. Or they lie about themselves and their experience and carry on a pretense of spiritual perfection.

Perfectionism will also hurt other relationships. The demanding, unrealistic standards perfectionists hold make them difficult people to be around. They are rule-keepers, list-makers, time-watchers, exacting and judgmental in terms of performance. The perfectionist is intolerant of failure in others because he is intolerant of failure in himself. The irony is that the impossible standards perfectionists impose on everyone around them are the very standards that they themselves cannot successfully manage. They drive people away, pressuring their wives, children and friends. Even in play they are demanding and exceedingly caught up in winning.

Perfectionism will alienate us from those we love. We cannot be vulnerable because to admit weakness when we struggle so with self-esteem is impossible for us. Some perfectionists I've known have dealt with the fact that they have no friends by claiming it is the price to pay for living at a level that is a cut above everyone else. It is lonely at the top. This is the height of emotional denial. It is a defense mechanism that warps reality. It is the twisted reason of one who lives in deep fear of being exposed.

Perfectionism can also destroy the fellowship of the church. The perfect church on this earth is an ideal, a wish dream that does not exist. It is not found anywhere in the New Testament, nor is it promised there. God's real church is a gathered fellowship of sinners living under the grace and forgiveness of Christ. Our unity in the church is a unity based on Christ's forgiveness. Our unity was not achieved by the unanimous consent of all believers to a perfect statement of faith or by the achievement of perfect morality among the saved. We are one because we are all sinners forgiven by a gracious God.

Pharisaism is always a problem for the serious Christian. If Christians did not care about their faith, they would never make the mistake of the Pharisee. At the heart of Pharisaism is a judgmental spirit concerned primarily with consistent performance according to the details of the Law.

The perfectionistic Christian is particularly vulnerable to the sin of the Pharisee. He is quick to see how everyone else falls short. He has a gift for being able to look past the railroad tie in his own eye and see the splinter in his brother's eye. His vocabulary is filled with "oughts" and "shoulds" when he talks about the church. He has the clearest idea (the more biblically astute conception) of what the church should be like. He knows how Christians ought to behave and what books they should read, and he is clear on every major doctrine and on most minor ones as well. He tests those he meets and works with on the basis of his doctrinal clarity. He fellowships only with those he judges to be at a worthy level. This is why he moves through the church from relationship to relationship. People always let him down.

His ideal of what the community ought to look like becomes the evaluative grid that filters everything he sees. You will hear him talk openly about the way things should be. The youth group is not good enough. The pastor's sermons are not good enough. The outreach of the church is not good enough. The adult classes lack quality teachers, the right topics are not being taught, and the wrong topics that are being taught are not being presented in the right way. Instead of being thankful for the church as a gift from God, for men and women who are willing to admit their faults and live under grace, doing what they can to share their lives in love one with another, the perfectionistic Christian holds his ideal church above the real church and judges God's fellowship on the basis of his dream. Instead of thankfully participating in the church as it really is, he demands that the church become what he thinks it ought to be. He loves his ideal more than he loves God's true community. This kind of wishful thinking will destroy the fellowship.

Dietrich Bonhoeffer saw such idealism as an enemy of the gospel. In *Life Together* he writes:

God hates visionary dreaming; it makes the dreamer proud and pretentious. The man who fashions a visionary ideal of community demands that it be realized by God, by others, and by himself. He enters the community of Christians with his demands, sets up his own law, and judges the brethren and God Himself accordingly. He stands adamant, a living reproach to all others in the circle of brethren. He acts as if he is the creator of the Christian community, as if his dream binds men together. When things do not go his way, he calls the effort a failure. When his ideal picture is destroyed, he sees the community going to smash. So he becomes, first an accuser of his brethren, then an accuser of God, and finally the despairing accuser of himself.[9]

Becoming aware of and determining to give up our perfectionism toward our Christian brothers and sisters and toward the
church may be a difficult battle. Our faith is so important to us.
It is supreme in our lives. If nowhere else, then surely in the
church of our perfect God we ought to be able to realize our
ideal.

The irony is, God does not seem to be as interested in producing the perfect community as we are. He appears to be more
concerned with building character. He seems very interested in
whether we can love, forgive and accept a brother who falls far
short of what we think he ought to be. He seems very interested
in whether we are truly thankful for the community in which
he has placed us and whether we can enter in and participate
with that community as a fellow struggler under grace. He
seems most interested in whether we realize the depth of our
own sinfulness and turn to him to experience repeatedly the joy
of forgiveness in Christ. For this is the beginning of true wisdom. This is the beginning of true community in Christ.

To quote Bonhoeffer again, "Every human wish dream that
is injected into the Christian community is a hindrance to genuine community and must be banished if genuine community
is to survive. He who loves his dream of a community more
than the Christian community itself becomes a destroyer of the
latter, even though his personal intentions may be ever so honest and earnest and sacrificial."[10]

*Another price we pay for perfectionism is that we often pass the curse
on to our children.* It is a cycle which is not easily broken. Perhaps your father was a perfectionist—demanding, critical, cool.
To win his love you worked to produce at a level that would
please him. Now you continue to place demands on yourself
that your father placed on you as a child. And you are demanding of your own children in the same way.

It is a strange phenomenon but commonly observed in family systems. As adults, we tend to act the same way our parents

acted. Sons of alcoholic fathers often become alcoholics. Physically or sexually abused children often abuse their own children. We appear to do this as a way of trying to prove to ourselves that our parents behaved correctly toward us. We are desperate to reconcile how we were treated with the idea we hold deep within us that our parents must have loved us. We convince ourselves that they treated us the way they did for our own good. We live out that conviction by re-enacting their parenting style in our own families. In this way destructive family patterns continue to dominate from generation to generation.

Young children are wonderfully free and fun to watch. I vividly remember Jana working on standing up in her playpen when she was still a baby. I was fascinated with the struggle. She would get a little way up, gripping the mesh walls and pulling with all her might. Then she would topple over and tumble into a ball at the center of the mat. Once on her hands and knees again, she would crawl to one of the sides and start the painful process all over again.

I watched her for at least a half hour, pulling with all the strength she had in her baby arms and pushing up on wobbly legs. Finally, by sheer accident, she got a good angle that offered some leverage. The next instant she was standing up in her playpen for the first time. Her face burst into a wide smile.

There was a refreshing freedom in her total disregard for repeated failures. It is this kind of freedom to try and fail that we hope will continue in our children as they grow and mature in our families. Kids have to be free to fail. How will they learn to make effective decisions without making some bad ones along the way? How will they build their skill levels for effective living if we never allow them the freedom to mess up?

The truth is, if God is going to do something new in you or in me, or in our children, we must necessarily be attempting something which has not been done before. And there are no guarantees regarding the outcome of these adventures in

Christ. What our world needs more than anything else today is Christian men and women who are courageous enough to reach for the potential of the new, even at the risk of failure.

This is where our perfectionistic tendencies can do damage to our kids. As parents, it is easy to create the mistaken impression in our children that our love for them is dependent upon their perfect performance. The idea is communicated when we excessively praise them for their "good" work, rewarding them with love and approval and then either criticize or ignore them when they make mistakes or produce an inferior final product.

This is where our children begin to get themselves and their work mixed up. When we praise their good work—which makes them feel good—without intending to do so we make them feel bad and rejected when they do work that we do not praise in the same way. Our emphasis on performance as parents creates a great tension in our children. They become afraid to risk, to reach out, to try new things. Our children learn that by playing it safe they can avoid the risk and pain of failure. If they don't try, they cannot fail. But by playing it safe, they can never develop their potential and live at the highest level possible for themselves and for Christ.

As perfectionists, we tend to measure our worth on the basis of our performance and achievement. This creates another problem in our parenting. We can easily slip into evaluating our worth as parents by the performance of our children. Think of the pressure this can put on kids to perform. Our high standards and our reactions of disapproval and frustration when the kids don't live up to them creates tremendous anxiety in the family. The kids are more likely to fail when they have to carry this enormous tension about their performance in school, or sports, or the arts, or their Christian lives. They try too hard. We see the stress and worry about it as parents, believing it must come from their failure. It reinforces our perfectionistic belief that failure is bad, dangerous and undesirable. We put even more pressure on them to perform. It creates more and greater stress. I have been close to a half dozen teen-age suicides in the past ten years that had the components of this tense scenario.

Judie tried to point out to me when the kids were younger that I treated our biological child, Gabe, differently than our adopted children. I denied it at first, but after we talked I became more aware of what I was doing. It was true. I seemed perfectly willing to let our adopted kids develop at their own pace in the areas of their giftedness. But Gabe was different. He had to be somebody, and he had to be the somebody I had in mind. It was puzzling to me. Why did I act this way?

In some sense our biological children are a kind of judgment on our genes. Whether my son makes it or not says something about who I am and my parenting. If I am perfectionistic, the achievement of my child is very important to me. If he doesn't do well, I must be a bad parent. But with our children in whom I was not biologically invested, I was relaxed and able to let them be themselves and explore life openly. They were more free to fail and to change direction. I did not feel the need to pressure them to conform to my preconceived standards. This was a real eye-opening experience for me.

What we want in our homes is a permission-giving climate. It is true that "perfect love drives out fear" (1 Jn 4:18). We can learn as fathers to shift the focus of our praise and encouragement toward recognizing the good attempts our children make instead of always concentrating on the quality of their finished product or achievements. I would rather have my children struggle with a difficult paragraph or painting or household chore that is a bit beyond their abilities, and not be able to finish it perfectly, than to have them choose something simple each time that they can finish easily.

When Jana was in ninth grade, she received a "D" in math the second quarter, after putting in a good effort. I talked with her and her teacher and counselor. Everyone admitted that she could easily get an "A" in the lower math section if she transferred. But Jana did not want to change classes. She asked her teacher if he would be willing to give her time on the mornings before tests and exams to help clear up sections she didn't understand. He said he would. Jana got a "B" in math the third quarter by hanging in there and putting in the extra time with her teacher. I was glad she risked it; yet I would have loved her and been proud of her even if she had failed to improve her grade.

Irreparable damage is caused in our families when we give the impression that we are just waiting for the next failure to occur so we can say, "I told you so." This is equivalent to saying, "I knew all along you couldn't do it. You are a failure." This is a permission-withholding climate. A child who grows up in this kind of climate lives in continual fear and discouragement. This is the kind of environment that produces the most compulsive perfectionists.

In our Christian homes, our kids should see that Mom loves Dad even when Dad's performance is less than perfect. And then they should see Mom reaching out, able to risk the challenge of something new because she is so thoroughly and completely loved by Dad and by God. The home should be a place where love is never contingent on perfect performance. And the home should be a place where forgiveness is granted willingly and eagerly, and never withheld. Forgiveness is a gift that we should all experience often. Forgiveness frees us from our need to be perfect. Once freed we do not have to spend so much time trying to make ourselves look like perfect people. Instead, we can be vulnerable, honest and open with each other. This is what it means to love in truth. We know the real people who live in our families, their problems, their shortcomings, and we love them as they are. This is the freedom that can live in the Christian family.

We can all learn to more easily accept the fact that we are imperfect, and not dwell on this. Our homes can be filled with grace, love and forgiveness. When they are, we create an environment in which our children can come to know God as he really is—a loving and forgiving Father.

So we see that the man who is a perfectionist is unsettled within, struggles with his relationships with friends, coworkers and family, and has difficulty relating to God and the church. Who will rescue him from this difficult entrapment?

Perfectionism and the Gospel of Grace

Perfectionism is the drive to prove to others that we are worthy to be loved. Somewhere along the way we begin feeling that we will only be loved if we can accomplish well the tasks of life. Someone important to us has made it clear through words or actions that love is granted on the basis of what we achieve. If we are never freed from this curse, we will spend our entire lives trying to earn the love of those who are important to us.

God has a different approach. He says through Paul that we are all equal in one important aspect; we are all sinners and fall short of the glory of God (Rom 3:23). But God's story doesn't end there. He looks at us, all of us, sinners in deep need, and he loves us. When Jesus wanted us to know his Father in heaven, he told the story of the Prodigal Son (Lk 15:11-32).

God is our Father. He loves us even if we have hurt him and chosen to go our own way. He wants us to come home. Instead of making it hard for us to return to fellowship with him, he makes it easy. He welcomes us home and invites us in. Jesus said: "Here I am! I stand at the door and knock. If anyone hears my voice and opens the door, I will come in and eat with him, and he with me" (Rev 3:20). And Jesus was known for eating with sinners. He is the Lord of love, forgiveness, grace and the Lord of the second chance.

Where in these pictures do we see a God eager to catch us in some sin, ready to take pleasure in punishing us for every mistake that shows we fall short of his holiness? Where is the God who records how many quiet times we have had this week, how many times we have witnessed, how many days we have fasted, how many hours we have studied his Word? Where in these pictures is the God of the push and shove, who demands more and more hours of running for Jesus on faster and faster spiritual treadmills? No, this is the God of the perfectionist, not the gracious, saving God of the Bible.

The apostle Paul agonizes over his inability to live up to the standard of the Law (Rom 7:14-25). But then God clears the apostle's mind, and Paul grasps and expresses the truth of grace. He writes, "Therefore, there is now no condemnation for those who are in Christ Jesus, because through Christ Jesus the law of the Spirit of life set me free from the law of sin and death" (Rom 8:1).

Grace sets us free. We do not have to earn God's love. He accepts us as we are and loves us more than we could ever love ourselves. When you begin to feel that God could not love you because you are a failure, meditate on Romans 5:7-8. "Very rarely will anyone die for a righteous man, though for a good man someone might possibly dare to die. But God demonstrates his own love for us in this: While we were still sinners, Christ died for us." Give up trying to earn God's love. You cannot do it. God's love is a free gift given to imperfect people like you and me. Let God love you. It is the only way to be truly free.

Once we give up our impossible craving for perfection and begin to live freely as a sinner loved by God and living under grace (Rom 5:1-2), we will find ourselves growing in our willingness to risk new challenges. The pressure is off. I am forgiven, and I can be forgiven again. I am free to fail. And God still loves and forgives me when I do. He accepts me even if

I'm not perfect. Now I can get on with growing to maturity in Christ, living in forgiveness and granting forgiveness to others, living under the graceful love of our loving Father in heaven and granting graceful love to family, neighbors and friends.

Learning to Love Our Imperfections

Perfectionism is as difficult to deal with as any other obsession. Gaining ground usually requires changing both our thinking and our instinctive responses to the experiences we encounter in life.

Several years ago I told the staff I worked with in Boulder that I was going on a program of planned irresponsibility. I explained that I felt I was entirely too earnest about work. I was coming in too early, going home too late, attending too many evening meetings. I started going to the YMCA in the mornings and getting more exercise. I took more time off. I worked at not being so obsessive and compulsive about my performance. I worked at being more accepting of the mistakes of others, and more relaxed about time-lines and startups and more flexible and realistic in my planning. There was a difference in the way those around me related with me and worked for me. The atmosphere was more relaxed, and there was more fun in the work. What surprised me most was that the quality of our team efforts was not reduced. The only thing we gave up was the push and shove that came from me and often created tension.

Most of my early drive and perfectionism resulted from my eagerness to please others as I developed early in my career. I wanted to prove myself. So I spent long hours working on the finest details of everything that touched my area of responsibility. In the middle of one particularly tough year I was asked to give a talk to preschool fathers about priorities. I accepted. During my preparation, I looked over my schedule from the beginning of January to the twenty-first of February. I had been out thirty-eight nights in that period of less than two months.

I put my schedule on an overhead transparency and did no further preparation. The next evening I showed my schedule to that group of young fathers and asked them for help. "What am I doing wrong?" I asked. We had an excellent time together discussing the drive of perfectionism, the pressures of our work situations, the need to feel important. But I left that night knowing that I would never again be away from my family thirty-eight nights in a fifty-one-day period.

There is a subtle lack of faith operating in much of our work in the evangelical church. We seem to believe that God cannot do it without us. Psalm 127:2 says, "In vain you rise early and stay up late, toiling for food to eat—for he grants sleep to those he loves." It is the Lord's work, whether providing food and shelter for our family, or reaching the world with his good news. He does give us real responsibility in the church, but the ultimate responsibility is never on our shoulders. We can rest and enjoy peace knowing that he is in charge. God's people are not to look driven and compulsive. We are not to carry excessive worry and tension (Mt 6:25-34). We are to be at peace because the God of peace never sleeps. He is able to guard his work and see that his sovereign ends are accomplished in the world.

There are some practical things you can do if you are perfectionistic that might help you to learn to love and celebrate imperfection. I have repeatedly gone through many of these steps myself trying to change the way I think about the things I attempt in life.

First, rethink what it means to be successful. It might help to remember, for instance, that a .300 hitter in baseball is a very good batter. But this average means that he gets a hit only three times in every ten times at bat. Some of us are trying to hit a home run every time we swing the bat. This is unrealistic. It will drive us crazy. We can lower our expectations and still produce at an acceptable level without driving ourselves wild chasing an impossible dream.

If you take a close look at what you are doing to yourself and others as a perfectionist, you may decide that the disadvantages of compulsive perfectionism far outweigh the advantages. Actually make a list of positives and negatives in your life that come from your perfectionism and weigh the results. My guess is that if you make such a list you will find the negatives far outweigh the positives. This can be a starting place for giving up perfectionistic actions and attitudes you have always thought of before as good.

Take time to think about some of the perfectionistic tendencies mentioned earlier in this chapter. Think about what might be wrong with the all-or-nothing attitude toward activities or projects. Write down your thoughts. Do you see the unrealism in this line of thinking? Was the whole day a complete zero because you missed one appointment?

Think of how your upbringing might have contributed to your perfectionism. How do you feel about yourself? Be honest. Do you struggle with self-esteem? Are you trying to win the love and acceptance of others by performing perfectly? Are you trying to win God's love this way?

Do you judge yourself critically for each and every mistake you make? Is your vocabulary filled with "shoulds" and "oughts" when it comes to evaluating how you've done? For several days write down your self-critical thoughts. Apply reason to these criticisms and see if you are justified in being so hard on yourself. Does your friend really think less of you as a person because you could not get away for lunch when it was convenient for him? How do those around you respond when you make a mistake? Do they judge you and put you down? Or do they feel more comfortable around you if you occasionally mess up? It may surprise you that people usually feel better about you when they see that you make mistakes just like they do.

Learning to set lower standards is significant for overcoming perfectionism. If we really measure the objective difference, it makes to achieve 97% over 92% on a report or project, we may soon be convinced that the extra work required to get to the 97% is probably not justified. Some work tasks have very little room for error. Here I'm thinking about those of you who might work in computer programming on sensitive and complex projects, or programs like aerospace that require the finest calculations to assure human safety and a successful mission. The thing to remember, though, is that everything in life does not have to be accomplished at the same level in order to bring satisfaction. It is unrealistic to be the best at everything and to demand 100% of yourself in all that you attempt. If some sport is really not your gift, but you enjoy participating, then join in and forget about becoming a top-rated player.

Another important aspect to consider in setting lower goals is that you will probably find that you work better under less pressure. The key is to set a reasonable goal that will create a sense of challenge but not be overwhelming. You can always go beyond your goal if you are able. Achieving the reasonable goal will give you a sense of satisfaction. If you go beyond the goal, that can be satisfying as well. The problem with perfectionistic goals is that they are so high that they create great stress. The stress is counterproductive in the work environment. This is why so many perfectionists do not achieve with consistency in their work or sports at as high a level as even less talented peers who are not perfectionistic.

One more thing that might help you is to set time limits on the things you do. I mentioned earlier that in preparation for teaching I used to study every available minute until I presented the material. I have learned though that there is a point of diminishing returns on time spent in preparation. Twice as much time given in study will not give you a presentation that is twice as effective. So I chose to limit my preparation time. I simply forced myself to stay away from the task until I reached the scheduled time for preparation. I have even gotten to the place now that I can really relax and not even think of the preparation until it is time to produce. Earlier I had to force myself not to study ahead of time and I carried anxiety. But as I stayed with my goals and saw that my teaching and preaching was apparently as helpful and effective as before, I gained a sense of peace toward that process which had before always created great stress. There is such a thing as too much time put into something. If you are perfectionistic, you will need to work on seeing the truth of this and measuring your involvement accordingly.

Perhaps you can become addicted as I have to achieving in the above-average range rather than trying to be extraordinary in everything. With perfectionism, shooting for the top in every attempt usually translates into less productivity and because of the stress of unrealistic goals, often produces work of lower quality. The rewards of greater peace, less stress, more available time, and the consistent productivity of good quality work can help us to learn to love imperfection.

Perfectionism is similar to many of the other temptations. It can become an obsession. When rationalization and denial take place, we need help to break through and gain control of our lives. Most of us are perfectionistic in some area. We will find that reading a chapter like this can help us to work on overcoming our tendencies that create tension for ourselves and for others. But if you are driven by perfectionism, you may need to seek outside help—particularly for perfectionists who think they can do it alone. Perfectionism is a complex obsession that is deeply rooted in your history. To unravel the influences that have contributed to your perfectionistic behavior, see a well-trained professional who has experience dealing with perfectionism and understands the spiritual dimensions involved.

Accepting God's Love

We will make little headway with this obsession unless we are

able at some point to accept the fact that God loves us completely and unconditionally just the way we are. The simple truth is,
there is nothing we can do that will make God love us any more
than he does right now. That's the whole story.

Think of the apostle Peter, of his repetitive failure, his consistent dullness in processing and understanding what his Lord
was teaching him, even his blatant denial of the Lord he loved
and his cowardice, fear and hesitancy in the days following the
crucifixion. And then, after the resurrection, on a lonely beach,
he again met the Lord he loved.

When Jesus said, "Peter, feed my sheep," Peter put it all together. Yes, Jesus knew who he really was, a miserable sinner
and failure, but he loved him and trusted him. When Jesus said,
"Feed my sheep," Peter heard him saying: "I know you, Peter,
everything about you. And I love you. And I trust you with my
most important work. Build my church."

Peter realized that Jesus was not fixated on perfect performance. Jesus was not going to hold his imperfections against him.
How freeing this realization must have been. Think of it, a
forgiven failure entrusted with the keys of the kingdom of God.
Peter no longer had to pretend to be more adequate, more
effective than others. From that day forth he was a new man
in Christ. He was freed to take responsible risks for his master.
He still failed and even had to be reprimanded by Paul on one
occasion. But he was able to move beyond failure because he
realized the freedom of being loved in truth, unconditionally,
and the power active forgiveness has in a believer's life.

Until we open our hearts and let God love us, accepting his
great gift of forgiveness through Christ, we will be like Peter on
the night our Lord was betrayed, enveloped in feelings of failure, discouragement and self-condemnation. We will be of no
use to anyone.

But Jesus comes to each of us. He lifts our faces and looks
into our eyes and deep into our hearts. "Let me love you," he

says. "I know all about you. I know your imperfections, your painful memories, your hidden thoughts, your hopes, your fears. You don't have to pretend anymore. Stop trying to be good enough to earn my love. I already love you more than you can even imagine. Now let me live my life through you."

It takes great courage to accept the fact of our imperfection, to accept the fact of our need for a Savior, and to turn our lives toward Christ. It means admitting that we cannot do it on our own. Giving up is the first step to renewal and a new life of peace in Christ. Pray that you will be able to accept God's unconditional love. And pray that you will be a person who grants love, grace and forgiveness to others.

It will make all the difference in your life.

Questions for Groups and Individuals

1. This chapter opens with a quotation from Chesterton, "Anything that's *really* worth doing is worth doing badly." What do you think Chesterton meant by this? Do you agree or disagree? Why?

2. According to the traits listed in the section "Anatomy of a Perfectionist" (pp. 168-69), how would you place yourself on the spectrum below?

Not At All Perfectionistic	Highly Perfectionistic

3. Name one area of your life in which you tend toward perfectionism. Name one area in which you are much more relaxed. Why do you think these two areas are so different for you?

4. How do you explain the difference between striving for excellence and the drive to be perfect? How do you draw the line between the two?

5. What harmful effects can perfectionism have on our spiritual lives? our relational lives? our family lives?

6. Do you think you inherited or learned perfectionism from your parents? Explain.

7. Do you see perfectionistic tendencies in your children? What are some practical ways you can help them avoid or overcome these tendencies?

8. What specific changes will you try to make on the basis of reading and studying this chapter?

8/DELIVERANCE

Then we cried out to the Lord,
the God of our fathers,
and the Lord heard our voice
and saw our misery, toil and oppression.
So the Lord brought us out of Egypt
with a mighty hand
and an outstretched arm,
with great terror and with
miraculous signs and wonders.
He brought us to this place
and gave us this land,
a land flowing with milk and honey.
DEUTERONOMY 26:7-9

Our God is a God who delivers.

The biblical account from the beginning of Genesis to the end of Revelation is an account of the work of our mighty God, the faithful deliverer. Throughout our history, God has been setting us free, releasing us from bondage, delivering us from slavery. In the midst of misery we can expect the miraculous. Every work of his mighty hand aims at a single end—to move us from death to life. God wants us to possess the land, the land flowing with milk and honey.

It is easy to lose sight of the fact that God wants to make us free men. Sin clouds the vision. Our toil makes us weak. We might even be so foolish or confused as to cling to our bondage instead of crying out to God for deliverance. There is a twisted security in slavery. Remember how often the Israelites looked back, argued with Moses that it would be better to return to Egypt than face the uncertainties of life with God. How often have we turned back on the road to the promised land? It is more appealing to our human side to walk by sight. God wants us to walk by faith.

Or we might lose hope because God's timing makes no sense to us when we're in deep pain. We have cried out for deliverance but we are still in Egypt, held in the grip of some powerful bondage. We know we cannot will our freedom. We need the power of God to be free. Yet God is silent. He sees our misery. He sees our toil. But has he heard our cries? If he has heard us, he has not acted. Why has he not stretched out his mighty hand and with signs and wonders delivered us from our oppression?

Pain is more powerful than memory. The agony of a present pain can make us forget how God has faithfully acted in the past. It takes another kind of miracle at times like these for God to remind us of who he is, the God of love, and of what he has faithfully accomplished in our lives and in the lives of his covenant people throughout biblical history. It takes another kind of will for us to choose to let God in at the point of our pain, to let him hold us and share in our suffering as we move through it. Remembering who God is and what he has done can help us to rest and trust as we sit in the waiting room of the great physician.

Peter has insight into this mystery. He writes: "Humble yourselves, therefore, under God's mighty hand, that he may lift you up in due time. Cast all your anxiety on him because he cares for you . . . And the God of all grace, who called you to his eternal glory in Christ, after you have suffered a little while, will himself restore you and make you strong, firm and steadfast. To him be the power for ever and ever. Amen" (1 Pet 5:6-7, 10-11). Peter knows that suffering offered to God becomes God's divine work. Pain is unredemptive in our lives only if we refuse to offer it to God. Pain fired in the crucible of faith brings forth God's glory.

I remember walking out of the delivery room by Judie's side as they rolled her down the hospital corridor. She was lying face down. She held our new son, Gabriel, in her hands, in front of her face. He was wrapped in a flannel baby blanket. Judie's cheek rested lightly on him like a kiss. He was quiet, warm, lovely. She was pale, empty, weary. The labor had been intense. Twenty-four hours of pain preceded the birth. I was astonished when she turned toward me, looked up, smiled and said, "Let's do it again."

An hour earlier she might have done almost anything to find relief from her pain. But now, resting her cheek on the glory that had been revealed, knowing the miracle that turns pain to joy, she was ready to face it again. She did not even have to think it over. She knew in no uncertain terms that it was worth it. All of it. This is not masochism. It is the apprehension of a deep and glorious mystery that escapes those who turn away from God. The mystery revealed is that God will fashion his glory from pain.

God will take the pain of this world and make it work redemptively according to his eternal purposes (Rom 8:28). Pain in the hands of our deliverer God brings the blessing of new life. He did it at the cross. There the suffering and death of his only Son made new life possible for every one of us. God will fashion new life from your pain as well. And when his glory is revealed, you will not question his wisdom.

Do You Want to Be Healed?
The Gospel of John records the story of Jesus' encounter with

an invalid at the pool of Bethesda (Jn 5:1-14). The sick and lame who came daily to the pool believed an angel's presence occasionally disturbed the surface of the water and anyone fortunate enough to enter the water first when the surface rippled could be healed of any infirmity. This man Jesus talked with had been lying by the pool for thirty-eight years. Jesus asks, "Do you want to get well?" The question is significant.

Two things often stand in the way of our deliverance. One barrier is denial, our determined refusal to admit we are sick. The other common deterrent is what lies behind Jesus' question of the man by the pool. Did he really want to be healed? Often we do not. We pretend that we do. But we are really afraid to risk new life. We can find comfort in our pains and problems. Our sins are like old friends. Can we leave the secure bondage of Egypt and risk the wilderness leading to the promised land?

The man at the pool had a pure heart. He answered well Jesus' penetrating question. He knew he was sick. There was no denial. And he yearned for healing. He told Jesus that. But he lacked the means to move to the pool when the water was stirred. Jesus had heard enough. He commands the paralyzed man to get up, pick up his mat and walk. The cure was instantaneous.

If we are to be delivered, we have to want it. Are you honestly in this place? Can you even admit your struggle, admit that something has enslaved you and holds you in its power? At a recent men's conference I spoke on temptation. A man receiving help with sexual addiction talked about his progress. He pointed out that many of the things I was saying made sense to him now that he was making headway against his addiction, but he felt strongly that he would have heard and understood little of it during the dark time of his early bondage and obsession.

Bondage creates spiritual blindness. Paul talks about this

kind of blindness in Romans 1:21-32. Men who could be healed
turn away from God and are darkened in their thinking and in
their hearts. They take part in every kind of wickedness and
depravity until they not only do evil, living in sin, but they
approve of and encourage those who practice evil as they do
(Rom 1:32). Snared in a deep and growing bondage we will
return again and again to a particular sin until it seems normal,
even right, to us. Held in the grip of the sin, we build defense
mechanisms to protect ourselves from the pain of guilt. This
dulls our consciences and drives God far from us. Soon we
"approve" of the behavior and even promote it. This is why it
is hard for us to receive spiritual insight when we have given
ourselves progressively to any sinful obsession. Our rationalization and denial are powerful and blinding.

The fact that you are reading this book suggests that you have
not progressed in your sin to this difficult place. Even though
you may struggle against something powerful, you still realize
that things are not right, not the way they should be or you
would probably have had no interest in opening these pages.
Thank God if you know your struggle. There is great hope in
God for those who know they need him.

"Do you want to be healed?" It is a penetrating question. We
love our sins in a way. Perhaps you feel like Augustine who
once said, "Lord make me chaste, but not yet." No, you know
this will not work. We harm ourselves by clinging to the security
of our sin. The sin robs us from the spiritually delicious experience of tasting the joy of glory that is to be ours. Lewis puts
it in perspective when he writes: "We are half-hearted creatures, fooling about with drink and sex and ambition when
infinite joy is offered us. Like an ignorant child who wants to
go on making mud pies in a slum because he cannot imagine
what is meant by the offer of a holiday at the sea, we are far
too easily pleased."[1]

It is by faith that the Israelites stepped toward the Red Sea, not knowing how they would be delivered by their deliverer God, not knowing the glory of the promised land or God's timing in leading them to it. They faltered, they struggled, they turned away from God in their weakness, but he was faithful. We can look back and see it now. This can strengthen our faith, enabling us say, "Yes, Jesus, I want to be healed, to know your glory yet to be revealed in me."

Our part to play in the process is to discern how best to put ourselves in the place where we can receive God's healing grace. We keep on stepping toward the water. As we step forward in faith, God steps with us. Biblical history convinces us that he is trustworthy. God delivers.

Stepping toward the Water

The twelve step method of Alcoholics Anonymous is a tremendous tool for helping those of us who seek deliverance to keep stepping toward the water of God's healing grace. Unlike the paralytic by the pool, most of us can move when the surface of the water is stirred, putting ourselves in a place where God's grace can enter our lives. If you are serious about receiving lasting healing for something that has a grip on your life, study carefully this twelve-step process that has helped to bring lasting healing to millions. Risk admitting your sin to yourself and others. Risk entering into a group or counseling relationship that includes the steps outlined below. Risk choosing into an accountable relationship. Step toward the water and receive healing and comfort from our deliverer God.

As you read through the steps, put in place of the word *alcohol* the aspect of your life you want to face and eliminate with God's help:

The Twelve Steps of Alcoholics Anonymous

1. We admitted we were powerless over alcohol—that our lives had become unmanageable.

2. Came to believe that a Power greater than ourselves

could restore us to sanity.

3. Made a decision to turn our will and our lives over to the care of God as we understood Him.

4. Made a searching and fearless moral inventory of ourselves.

5. Admitted to God, to ourselves, and to another human being the exact nature of our wrongs.

6. Were entirely ready to have God remove all these defects of character.

7. Humbly asked Him to remove our shortcomings.

8. Made a list of all persons we had harmed, and became willing to make amends to them all.

9. Made direct amends to such people wherever possible, except when to do so would injure them or others.

10. Continued to take personal inventory and when we were wrong promptly admitted it.

11. Sought through prayer and meditation to improve our conscious contact with God as we understood Him, praying only for knowledge of His will for us and the power to carry that out.

12. Having had a spiritual awakening as the result of these Steps, we tried to carry this message to alcoholics, and to practice these principles in all our affairs.[2]

The Twelve Step Program has been so effective that it is used now in numerous groups to assist in the healing process for any addictive illness or lifestyle. Besides groups for alcoholics, there are now a growing number of good groups for those under the power of other chemical dependencies, eating disorders, emotional disturbances, sexual addiction, compulsive gambling, sexual and physical abusiveness. There are an equal number of helpful groups for those who live with parents and spouses who struggle with these illnesses and addictions. These groups provide a way to help stop the addictive behaviors and to begin building a healthy lifestyle.

The principles in the twelve steps work. But the power is not in the program. The twelve steps simply put us in a place where God can work his grace in our lives and bring about his peace, his freedom and his glory.

Biblical Principles behind the Program

Why does the twelve-step program work? The answer is that the foundational principles are consistent with biblical principles. And anyone leading a twelve step program like the one outlined above—even if the person is not a Christian—will emphasize that significant and lasting healing only comes when God is honestly invited into the process.

Perhaps the brief acronym HEALED will help to fix the steps in your mind.

Help!

Establish your life in God

Access accountable relationships

List harms, repent and amend

Enter into prayer

Dare to share

Help! Admit you need it. Be willing to ask for it. Knowing our powerlessness against the sin that controls us is an absolutely necessary first step toward lasting healing. The reason asking for help is so hard for us as men is that it sounds like we're admitting we can't handle it, we can't do it on our own. That's right. And we can't.

It is a significant surrender. As long as we persist in our attempts to manage sin in our own strength, we will remain under its power. This first step is a recognition of and a submission to the truth of our fallen condition and our total inability to overcome sinfulness through an act of our will. What we really need is to be healed. Does that mean we surrender and then do nothing? No, because by choosing to let God do his healing work, we also choose to cooperate with the divine physician as he prescribes our treatment and rehabilitation.

It is important to choose into our healing. Even medical doctors will tell us how necessary it is that a patient want to be healed. We have heard so often of men and women who die because they did not have the will to live. We die spiritually, too, when we refuse to submit ourselves to the divine healer and to fight for our spiritual lives. Part of our total surrender is to keep stepping toward God's grace. We cooperate with the Holy Spirit in the healing process. We seek to know and to do God's will.

You hate to go to the doctor, don't you? I do too. It doesn't feel very macho. It might be fine to resist going to the doctor when you've got a simple cold or the flu. But it is foolish to try to heal ourselves when we are suffering from a potentially terminal illness. It is just as foolish to refuse the healing power of Christ when we are suffocating in sin that will kill us. We cannot heal ourselves. The sooner we give this idea up, the quicker we will move on toward the wholeness and fullness God would have us enjoy in Christ.

Establish your life in God. The second of AA's twelve steps talks about the Power greater than us and the need to turn in faith toward that Power. We know as Christians who that Power is. His name is God the Father, God the Son, Jesus Christ, and God the Holy Spirit. The Bible makes it clear that there is no other name by which men receive salvation (Acts 4:12). This claim is made by Peter and John before the Sanhedrin. A man crippled from birth had been healed. They tell how the miracle occurred and explain the source for all healing when they say, "By faith in the name of Jesus, this man whom you see and know was made strong. It is Jesus' name and the faith that comes through him that has given this complete healing to him, as you can all see" (Acts 3:16). It is this same faith that comes through our relationship with Christ that can bring healing and wholeness to us today. Our relationship with God in Christ is established by faith as we turn toward his grace and believe in him and trust him to deliver us into newness of life.

Access accountable relationships. AA's steps three through seven ask us to turn our lives over to God, to address with great honesty our sinfulness and failures, and to admit our struggles and weaknesses to God and to another person. This is repentance with accountability. It is as James recommends when he writes, "Therefore confess your sins to each other and pray for each other so that you may be healed" (Jas 5:16). If we do these things, we will break through to the light. We reverse the dark, downward spiral into blindness and denial so powerfully described by Paul in the last section of Romans 1. We regain with this courageous honesty a new relationship with our deliverer God and a new willingness to let him build us from where we are to where he wants us to be. He cannot work in our lives as long as we persist in pretense, living a lie.

List harms, repent and amend. Steps eight and nine reunite us in fellowship with those we have harmed through our persistent sin. This bold action also helps to build a wider community of accountability. It is not likely that we are going to want to repeat this tough assignment often. And it is an effective way to authentically put our past behind us and move on.

The Devil wants us to be fixed at a particular point in our past. If he can accomplish this, we will make no progress with God. If we can be freed of the things in our past that grip us and keep us tied to earlier points in our development, we will begin to see new life and new strength. God says: " 'Their sins and lawless acts I will remember no more.' And where these have been forgiven, there is no longer any sacrifice for sin" (Heb 10:17-18). God forgives and forgets. Jesus is the lasting sacrifice that makes the repetitive Old Covenant sacrifices unnecessary. God's forgiveness through Christ thaws that frozen grip in which the mistakes and memories of the past imprison our minds and wills. Satan cannot hold us back if we let God's forgiveness rule. When Satan tries to freeze your progress by bringing up your past, you bring up to him his future. God has already freed you from the bondage of past sin. Live as a free man.

Maintaining a personal inventory and working to admit openly when we fail keeps us in a place where we can continually receive God's healing grace. This is why AA's step ten is important. If we close up, we return to the rationalization and denial that once impeded our progress. Deciding to live honestly with ourselves, God and others is an intentional choice we make to remain free and let God love and heal us.

Enter into prayer. Nothing is more important to building our relationship with God than prayer. Step eleven says that through prayer we gain wisdom and strength to overcome. James says we are to confess to each other and pray for each other because "the prayer of a righteous man is powerful and effective" (Jas 5:16). If you pray, expect a spiritual battle. The enemy knows the power of prayer. He will do anything to keep you from it. Persist in prayer and you will see the power of God at work in your life.

Dare to share. Step twelve in the AA process asks for a willingness to give help to others who struggle as you have struggled. A wonderful mystery of God's economy is that he wants to bring new life to others who are hurting in the midst of their struggles by healing you and using what you have learned to do his kingdom work. Out of your pain God can bring about glory in the lives of others. Nothing is wasted in God.

Paul writes, "Praise be to the God and Father of our Lord Jesus Christ, the Father of compassion and the God of all comfort, who comforts us in all our troubles, so that we can comfort those in any trouble with the comfort we ourselves have received from God" (2 Cor 1:3-4). God comforts you in your troubles with his love so that you can in turn comfort others who are similarly distressed. Once we were so caught up in our sin and depression that we could not see beyond ourselves. But now that we are receiving the healing grace of Christ and have grasped hope, we can share that hope with others. God delivers us from bondage. Now that we have been set free we announce to others and make the truth known through our love that there is hope and freedom in Christ.

There is nothing more meaningful that any of us can do than to extend the love and grace of Christ to another who is lost in sin. "Whoever turns a sinner from the error of his way will save him from death and cover over a multitude of sins" (Jas 5:20). It is a wonderful and powerful thing to help save the life of another. Our struggles are redeemed in kingdom work. In Christ we can see God's purposes behind our pain. Jesus' suffering on the cross was both purposeful and sacrificial. Our suffering, too, becomes sacrificial as we reach out with forgiveness and love to comfort others as we have been comforted with the grace, love and forgiveness of Christ. This is how we lay our lives down in Christ's name. God works in and through our pain to bring about his glory in our lives and in the lives of those with whom we share the practical love of Christ and the hope of eternal life.

That He May Lift Us Up

The Twelve Steps are effective and do put us in the place where God can best accomplish his work. But no earthly program alone will save or heal us. And we cannot predict how or when God will act to heal a particular need in our lives.

In C. S. Lewis's *The Chronicles of Narnia*, the lion, Aslan, represents Christ. One of the key aspects of the personality of Aslan mentioned throughout the books is that he is not a tame lion. He is not predictable. And our God is not a tame God. Just because he has acted a certain way in one person's life does not mean he will act the same way in another's, even when the circumstances seem identical to us. I have also caught myself feeling very sure that I know how God will act in a situation I'm facing today because he acted a certain way years ago when I faced something similar. But we cannot have this kind of certainty about God. God does not have to repeat himself. Every moment of our lives exists as a new opportunity for God to do in us his creative work of redemption and deliverance.

We have to learn to be receptive to God's new ways of working in us. That means that we learn to accept his will and his timing regarding our healing. I may have been delivered from the power of some bondage with a single earnest prayer at one moment in my life. At other times I may struggle with God in prayer for many years and not receive the same kind of deliverance. This is a deep mystery about the will and timing of God.

Once we choose to place ourselves in the hands of God, we need to rest in his grace. We will experience his deliverance. But are we willing to trust God's sovereign timing in his unique and personal ministry in our lives? Will we humble ourselves under God's mighty hand that he may lift us up in due time? (1 Pet 5:6). Will we accept God's unusual way of healing that requires us to live on in his strength with the broken thing still in our lives? God does not remove the thing that plagues us. Instead, his way is to overcome the evil power exerted by the sin in our lives through the life-giving, resurrection power of the cross.

This is how God heals. We are not to trust in our own power to control our drinking, our gluttony, our sexual sin. The alcoholic will always be an alcoholic. The glutton will always be tempted to overeat. The greedy man will battle his selfish desires throughout life. But by the power of God we can be strengthened to overcome the powerful bondage of our sin. We can make progress by growing in grace and letting God have more and more of us day by day. We can know the closeness and power of Christ to come against the powers of darkness in our lives.

Healing in Christ, then, takes on this different meaning.

Healing on the spiritual level does not fix the broken thing. We live with the brokenness, but we have victory over it because God overpowers sin's power that has held us captive. This is how he sets us free. The brokenness remains, but by God's power we are delivered to enjoy newness of life. What a tremendous testimony to God's grace. He delivers and sustains us. It is all God. We are weak, but he is strong. And even the powerful brokenness of physical death cannot hold us captive. Death itself is victoriously overpowered by God's mighty work in the cross of Christ. We were dead, but are now alive in Christ. We share in his resurrection.

It is because we experience pain that we seek deliverance. We would not seek God if it were not for the pain of our struggle. We can be thankful when our pain drives us to the mercy, comfort and love of our deliverer God. In him we find rest for our souls. Jesus extends this call to us: "Come to me, all you who are weary and burdened, and I will give you rest. Take my yoke upon you and learn from me, for I am gentle and humble in heart, and you will find rest for your souls. For my yoke is easy and my burden is light" (Mt 11:28-30). Jesus, our deliverer, invites us into this great freedom. Accept his grace, his will, his loving timing, his deep rest for your weary soul.

If we can remember two things, they will serve us well. The first is that nothing can separate us from God's love, not trouble or hardship or persecution, not even death (Rom 8:35-39). Paul understood this clearly. Even with all he had been through—the beatings, the stonings, the shipwreck, the attack and false accusations that came because he lived for the gospel—Paul knew the abiding love and strength of God, and he could not be stopped. He wrote, "We are hard pressed on every side, but not crushed; perplexed, but not in despair; persecuted, but not abandoned; struck down, but not destroyed" (2 Cor 4:8-9). We, too, will suffer if we belong to Christ. But we will also know his love that is deeper than our pain.

The second thing has been touched on earlier. We need to be reminded that the struggle is worthwhile. Paul also knew this deep wisdom. He writes, "I consider that our present sufferings are not worth comparing with the glory that will be revealed in us" (Rom 8:18). The pain is not worth comparing to the glory. The victory is ours in Christ. Place your present pain in the hands of God through prayer. Believe in the miracle of new life. Rest humbly in the mystery that God redeems suffering. By doing so, you allow his grace to work through your pain and bring about the glory to come.

Let us relish with Paul the truth that our God delivers his people from darkness to light, from death to life, from the weight of our pain to the glory that is to be revealed in us. Hear Paul again in 2 Corinthians 4:16-18:

> Therefore do not lose heart. Though outwardly we are wasting away, yet inwardly we are being renewed day by day. For our light and momentary troubles are achieving for us an eternal glory that far outweighs them all. So we fix our eyes not on what is seen, but on what is unseen. For what is seen is temporary, but what is unseen is eternal.

We suffer for a moment. The glory is forever. Fix your eyes on the glory.

Questions for Groups and Individuals

1. Have you in the course of your Christian journey had a powerful experience of God delivering you from a particular sin? If so, describe it.

2. The Bible teaches that people cannot free themselves from the sin in their lives. However, some would insist that they have succeeded in overcoming bad habits or behaviors on their own. How would you respond to this claim?

3. One thing that often stands in the way of our being delivered from sin is our inability or refusal to see our own sin. In the course of reading this book, were you confronted with some sin that you had previously failed to recognize? What was it?

4. Once a person recognizes his sin, what do you think are the essential steps he must take to become free? Are your steps different from the steps

listed for Alcoholics Anonymous?

5. How do you initially react to each of the steps toward healing discussed in the section "Biblical Principles behind the Program?" (p. 200) Which step do you think would be difficult for you to carry out? Why?

6. It can be said of temptation, "God does not remove the boulders from the rapids of life; he raises the level of the water." What do you think this means? How would you apply this word picture to your experience of how God has worked against temptation and sin in your life?

7. In what specific ways have you been comforted by this chapter on deliverance? In what specific ways have you been challenged?

9/HOW CAN I HELP MY MAN?
A CHAPTER FOR WOMEN

Relationships are like a dance,
with visible energy racing,
back and forth between partners.
Some relationships are the slow,
dark dance of death.
COLETTE DOWLING

God give us grace to accept with serenity
The things that cannot be changed,
Courage to change the things which should be changed,
And the wisdom to distinguish the one from the other.
REINHOLD NIEBUHR

*S*arah would not have come in on her own. A friend called me and asked if I had time to see someone very depressed about her life and marriage. I said yes.

Sarah came to my office the next afternoon. She was both physically sick and emotionally drained. She was suffering from a painful digestive disorder caused by excessive stress. We be-

gan together the process of untying the tightly knotted relationship she had been living in with her husband for twenty years,
a relationship that was getting progressively worse and causing
her greater and greater anxiety.

The marriage looks good on the outside. Mike is a successful
financial planner. His clients are also successful people. Mike
is good at making a lot of money for them and making a lot
of money for himself. Mike's huge home and two expensive
cars speak of his success. The home is well cared for, beautifully
decorated, set up for entertaining. Sarah handles that. Their
two children do well in school and are good in sports. They
dress well. They are well-behaved teen-agers in public.

Sarah's motto is "I know I can only change myself." She talks
about how through the years she has worked harder and
harder at being a better wife, a better mother. Keeping up the
huge house for entertaining is necessary to maintain the appropriate image for her husband's business. Sarah feels on call in
her own home because Mike is always surprising her by bringing business associates and clients in without notice. The home
has to be prepared at all times to receive these surprise guests.
Sarah keeps herself looking good, the house looking good, the
kids looking good, the marriage looking good. This is all necessary to keep the business looking good.

For the past two years her husband has been seeing another
woman. Sarah feels she has handled that well. She can only
change herself. She knows that. So she works harder at being
a good wife by forgiving him and at being a good mother by
covering up for him with the kids so they won't be hurt. She
makes him look good. Everything she does—from his laundry
and ironing to granting him a totally free personal schedule—
makes Mike attractive to others. It is good for business. It is
even good for his affair. A well-dressed, well-heeled man, who
does not have the burden of hassles at home, is a great find
for the other woman who is having all the fun money can buy

without any of the work that comes with keeping up a permanent relationship. The other woman has the good time; Sarah has the permanent relationship.

I asked Sarah what her home life was like as a child. She described without emotion the earlier years of living with her abusive, alcoholic mother. Sarah's father divorced her mother when Sarah was in elementary school. She made up her mind that when she married she would never get a divorce and cause that kind of pain for her children. Sarah as a young teen-ager did all the housework, cooked meals and worked outside the home several nights a week and on weekends to bring money into the family. She called in sick for her mother when she was too drunk to go to work. Sarah did her best to keep up the image, to keep up what was left of their little family. Her mother beat her at times, but more often abused her with hurtful words. The more she did to help in the house, the more her mother abused her. She tried harder and harder to win her mother's approval and love. Her mother's friends told her she was a beautiful, responsible, hard-working young woman. They wished their daughters could be more like Sarah.

The marriage is sick on the inside. Everything Sarah does to be a better wife and mother contributes to the destructive relationship. Separation or divorce are out of the question. She has made a decision about that. She will not hurt her children like she was hurt by her father. Mike knows she is committed to the marriage. He does not have to worry about Sarah bailing out on him and leaving him in a mess.

Sarah's image as a gifted and talented homemaker, decorator, entertainer and hostess brings her high compliments from friends and from Mike's business associates. She is talked about as the ideal wife and mother. This drives her perfectionism and affirms her work. It convinces her that she is doing the right thing. But Mike gives her no affirmation at all. Sarah tries harder to change herself, to be more forgiving, to come up with new ideas for supporting Mike in his work and in his social life, thinking that if she does an even better job, she will win his approval and get him back. The better she manages things, though, the harder he is on her.

The kids treat Sarah the same way Mike does. She lives for them as well, chauffeurs them around to their many activities, cleans up after them, keeps them looking good and entertains their friends. She is sure that they will someday appreciate what she has done for them. The kids do not know that Mike is having an affair. Sarah is careful not to argue with him in front of them. She would not want them to have to share in the pain she is going through because of the affair. On occasion, when there is tension between what one of the kids wants and what Sarah thinks would be best, Mike always sides with the children. This hurts and confuses Sarah.

Now Sarah is physically ill resulting from the emotional stress she has carried for years. Things have only gotten worse. Nothing is better. Sarah's level of stress is greater now than ever before. Her stomach cramps and intense pain keep her from performing at her accustomed level. She knows that she is not now able to manage everything at the level the other family members have learned to expect. If she can't do the one thing she is good at, keeping up the image, what will become of her?

When the Solution Becomes the Problem

Why do I tell you Sarah's story in a chapter on how to help your man? I hope you can see that there are complex dynamics that operate within the marriage relationship which sometimes make it difficult to bring real help and healing. I chose to tell this true story about Sarah because it illustrates so well a number of things that will not work if you really want to be a help to your man.

First, it will be impossible to bring any real help into a relationship if your behaviors only enable or encourage a problem in your marriage. Everything Sarah chooses to do makes it possible for Mike to continue his promiscuous behavior and abuse of the marriage relationship without having to experience the normal consequences of his actions. Sarah keeps the home looking good. She covers for Mike so the children will not find out the truth about their dad. Sarah manages everything for the household which frees Mike to use the home to enhance the business that supports his promiscuous lifestyle.

Sarah's behavior is deeply rooted in the patterns she learned while growing up with her mother. She worked herself nearly to death trying to win her mother's approval. Her competency was a threat to her alcoholic mother who would lose her temper over trivial things and beat Sarah or verbally abuse her. Sarah did not understand the dynamic, and after she was abused would work even harder to win her mother's love and approval. The better she got at managing the house—doing those things her mother could no longer do because of her drinking—the more her mother abused and mistreated her. Now she is doing the same thing with Mike. She is living out in her marriage a relationship which is almost identical to the relationship she had with her mother. Even Sarah's basic philosophy of life which concentrates on changing herself for the better is counterproductive in bringing health to the marriage. But Sarah has a hard time seeing why the good things she is doing only make matters worse.

There are numerous ways that you, like Sarah, might be enabling your husband's struggle with some problem or temptation. If you ignore or deny that he has a problem, for instance, there is little hope that progress will be made. Or you might be supporting his problem with denial by agreeing with his rationalizations, or contributing rationalizations of your own. It is often difficult to face the truth, especially when it means that facing the truth might make a radical difference in the way you live. It seems easier to put up with a problem you've gotten used to than to live through the transitional mess that might be created in trying to fix it.

Also common in relationships where there is enabling is the pattern of the wife taking on too much responsibility for the husband's behavior. This often occurs when the wife blames herself for her husband's problem. If her husband is having an affair, she feels it must be something she's done wrong. Sarah was driven by this dynamic. This self-blame creates the "I just need to try harder or change myself" attitude which puts all of the responsibility on one side of the relationship, and none of the responsibility on the person who really has to own the problem—the man engaging in the behavior. A husband learns quickly how to take advantage of his wife's guilt feelings. If the wife is vulnerable at this point, the husband will continue to blame her for his drinking, sexual misconduct, abusiveness or any struggle he may be having.

If you sense that there may be this kind of destructive enabling in your relationship, you may need to seek professional help to sort out the issues and find a way to bring a proper balance into your relationship. The key idea is this: at the point where your attempts to improve the relationship instead encourage and reinforce the behaviors you are hoping to change, you will have to find another strategy.

There is another way that the solution can become the problem. Many wives turn to manipulative techniques to try to change their husband's behavior. Some women nag. Others beg and bargain. Some try to control the relationship through explosive anger and public outbursts. These women are good at finding ways to hurt their husbands as they have been hurt. Others control more subtly with guilt and through clinging and pleading. And what makes things worse is the tendency in most people to use the same strategy each time a problem arises in the relationship. Their tendency is to stay with that particular strategy even when it becomes obvious that it is not working.

The wife nags her husband because of his overeating. He eats even more under the pressure of the nagging. So she nags him more. The more incessantly she nags him about the problem, the worse the problem gets.

If the solution has become the problem, you have to do something differently. They tell you in baseball if you're in a batting slump, change your stance. In his book *Love Must Be Tough* Dr. James Dobson speaks to the issue of how strategies aimed at controlling or manipulating another person are counterproductive in the relationship. He writes:

> The answer requires the vulnerable spouse to open the cage door and let the trapped partner out! All the techniques of containment must end immediately, including manipulative grief, anger, guilt and appeasement. Begging, pleading, crying, hand-wringing and playing the role of the doormat are equally destructive. There may be a time and place for strong feelings to be expressed and there may be an occasion for quiet tolerance. But these responses must not be used as persuasive devices to hold the drifting partner against his or her will.[1]

The way these clinging, smothering or controlling behaviors affect a relationship is by creating a growing lack of respect for the clinger that leads to diminished love. Manipulation or pleading will not renew love. You will want to learn how to love without smothering or controlling. True love must be tough. Learn how to truly let go and allow your man the freedom of having to deal with the real consequences of his choices. And this is not done out of spite. It is genuine love that sees this as the only way to find or rebuild health and respect in a troubled relationship.

Is there scriptural basis for this kind of letting go? Paul writes in 1 Corinthians 7:12-15: "If any brother has a wife who is not a believer and she is willing to live with him, he must not divorce her. And if a woman has a husband who is not a believer and he is willing to live with her, she must not divorce him. . . . But if the unbeliever leaves, let him do so. A believing man or woman is not bound in such circumstances; God has called us to live in peace." Paul saw that nothing is to be gained in a relationship by coercive tactics. Living in peace requires learning to let go. The act of authentically releasing another from your control is an act that takes great strength and courage. The important thing to see is that strength is communicated when this happens. I have watched men turn completely around because their wives make tough choices that communicate strength rather than clinging weakness. It is easier to love someone you respect than it is to love someone you can control.

There are no guarantees that freeing your spouse will automatically bring the love and health you seek in your relationship. But there is no other way to have authentic love. All enabling and controlling behaviors will only contribute to the problem. This is where my help for Sarah broke down. She refused every suggestion to try a new strategy for bringing about the change she hoped for in the relationship. She was too frightened of the possibility of losing Mike to step out of her enabling behaviors and let him experience the real consequences of his choices. All she was really interested in was finding a way to regain her physical health so she could maintain again the huge house as she was accustomed to doing. This relationship is the slow, dark dance of death. And Sarah, Mike and the kids are all dying in it.

If you think you might be enabling your husband's problematic behavior, get help from someone who understands these relational dynamics. You might learn more about your enabling tendencies from reading some current literature on the topic. *Codependent No More*, by Melody Beattie, has become a standard text in this field. Robin Norwood's *Women Who Love Too Much* is another helpful book.

It is extremely important for you to understand and begin dealing with your enabling tendencies if this is a problem for you. I have watched so many marriages break apart because a woman is not able to make the tough choices required to bring honesty into the relationship. The deeper sadness for me is watching these women become involved in another relationship later that has the same deathly dynamics. Women who do not learn to manage this aspect of their personalities repeatedly live out this dark scenario.

This is the major reason for my irritation with the doctrine of unqualified submission taught by so many Christians and churches today. The church is very good at producing submitted servants. And submission and servanthood are key aspects to living authentically as Christian men and women in our day. But nurturing abuse can never be a good strategy. There is no biblical warrant for this. Where submission and servanthood nurture sinful behavior, another strategy has to evolve. Situations like these require honest confrontation. Love must be tough at times, or it is not biblical love. We have to be strong enough to challenge those who need to be challenged to live responsibly according to the demands of love in the marriage relationship.

How Can You Help Your Man?

Women can bring effective help to men, but it is a sensitive issue. If the woman takes a helping posture, it naturally puts her in a one-up position with her man. This often has the effect of bringing the male ego into play. The man is thrust into the care-receiver role while the woman takes the care-giver role in the relationship. Pride can make it impossible for a man to receive from his wife the help he really needs.

It is common for men to refuse counseling because they are afraid they might find out their wives have been right all along. They are afraid to admit that they may have a problem. They retreat rather than risk being found out. Their egos require that they maintain the one-up position in their marriages. A man will get nowhere if he cannot find a way past this ego problem.

For your helping gestures to work, your man has to be as willing to receive help as you are to give it. He also has to know what he really needs. He might be hurting and reaching out, for instance, but be denying his real problem. If he cannot identify the real need and express in specifics what kind of help he wants, it will be hard for you to respond. Once you have a clear understanding of the real need, you will want to deliver the right amount of help, no more or less than your husband has asked for. Be careful here. Many wives anticipate what they think their husbands need and bring help where it is not needed or wanted, or they offer the wrong kind of help that does nothing for the real problem or struggle the husband faces.

You may, without thinking, try to give your husband what your mom always gave your dad when he was acting this way. This will shut the process down. Communication is so important here. If this happens, your husband will reject the help he hasn't asked for or that doesn't really meet his need. You may become angry because he has reached out to you and now he rejects you. He is further convinced that you are not really listening and is hesitant to trust you further. If you are answering questions he's not asking, or giving help he doesn't want or need, it will undermine his trust in you and close off communication. Without communication you will live in separate worlds. You will not be effective in helping one another.

It is supremely important to a truly healthy relationship that help be given and received in both directions. If your relationship gets stuck with you in the one-up role, unhealthy dependency develops. If you are to help your husband through some struggle or problem with temptation, then he should be allowed as well to help you through struggles and difficulties you may have. Sometimes it is ego fulfilling for us to play the care-giver role, but that same ego will not let us become a care-receiver. This creates an unhealthy imbalance in the relationship. When we can both give and receive help, there is true balance.

Foundational to this kind of reciprocal relationship is mutual trust. Trust is built on commitment and responsibility. You are supposed to be able to rely on me because I have promised myself to you in the marriage relationship. I ought to be able to rely on you for the same reason. We learn quickly, though, that there is more to developing real trust in one another than speaking our marriage vows. Trust is built in the relationship over time as our responses become predictably dependable.

As you predictably behave in a dependable manner, trust will grow in the relationship. When your husband risks exposing himself to you by sharing a difficult struggle, and he receives acceptance, encouragement and help, he will grow toward greater openness. You must learn to receive him as he really is rather than cling to a knight-in-shining-armor fiction that does not allow him the freedom to express his real struggles and temptations. Then you will build the trust that is essential for a quality relationship of mutual openness, forgiveness, accountability and support.

Are you prepared to hear what some of his real struggles are? It would be good for you to read about men and learn about men at every opportunity so you can understand more fully why we are different in many key areas and why certain things may have more power in our lives than they have in yours. This will help you to hear your husband's struggles without being shocked and without expressing judgment or criticism if he opens up to you an area of need.

I know a man who got up the courage to tell his wife that he struggled with temptation toward a younger woman in his office. His wife responded sharply, "How could you!" and turned away from him. Her response forced him to retreat from her and try to deal privately with the difficult temptation. The fact that he was quickly judged rather than loved and listened to by his wife made attraction to the other woman even more difficult to resist. It will be a long time before he opens up to his wife again. This woman was not prepared to respond appropriately to her husband's need. She missed a golden opportunity to open the door of intimacy a crack and let true growth and health into their marriage relationship. A man who has had the door slammed shut on his fingers will be careful not to put them in there again.

What If He Resists Help and Change?

What can you do if your husband is struggling but hides himself from you? What if he will not ask for help? Can you still bring help?

Some men lack the skill or awareness to know how to take the first steps toward authentic change. A man may be struggling with something he does not understand, or be in denial about his problem, or wrap himself in the impenetrable cocoon of his male ego, or be fanning his peacock feathers in an empty "I'm really strong" display. You may know very well what he needs, but he has isolated himself from you and the loving help you might be able to bring.

Prayer is so important in situations like these. You will want to seek the Lord's wisdom about how to communicate your availability without pressuring your husband or losing patience. James writes, "If any of you lacks wisdom, he should ask God, who gives generously to all without finding fault, and it will be given to him" (1:5). In the broader context of that verse James is saying that we need wisdom in order to make sense out of the trials we face, and that God will give us that wisdom if we persist in prayer. This is a great promise from God's Word that we are not left alone to depend on our frail human resources that are never adequate to resolve these relational dilemmas.

Concentrate in prayer on the wisdom needed to communicate effectively your love, friendship, availability. Pray also about the timing of your chosen interaction. You may be completely correct about your husband's problems and needs, but if your help is out of step with God's timing, you will only drive him more deeply into his defenses. If you judge or accuse or know-it-all, or quickly label your husband's problem, your attempts to bring any real help will be counterproductive.

Pray that your love for him will grow even when he makes this difficult because of the way he treats you. If he risks vulnerability, listen carefully. Don't jump in immediately with the solution you've been thinking about for weeks. Pray about your response. Show him that you are willing to pay the price of living through the difficult thing with him. Show him that you want to see and know his need from his point of view. Be empathetic. Only this kind of sensitive love can help him to break out of his cocoon and grow toward new life in Christ that will bring the healing and wholeness he may now not even know he needs.

Pray also that you may know and understand your motives clearly. Does your desire to see change in your husband spring primarily from your love that wants only what is best for him and for a healthy and reciprocal marriage relationship? Or do you want to bring about changes in his style or personality because it would make life easier for you? Are you really willing to let go and let God do the healing work, even if it means radical changes in your husband, and perhaps, radical changes in your present lifestyle? Do you want him to experience authentic change and growth in Christ or do you mainly want him to be the man you want him to be?

I wonder, for instance, if Sarah would be willing to really let God change Mike. What if Mike became a Christian, grew to the place where he started asking important lifestyle questions? What if he wanted to sell the big house, the fancy cars, get out of the country-club social circuit? Would Sarah be willing to let God have his way in Mike's life, or would she only be willing to accept change to a point?

Do we really want what is best for our spouses? Or do we just want things to go our way? Change is threatening to us. But if we can honestly trust God and rest in him, be truly open to whatever he may be doing in the lives of those we love, this flexibility will help create an environment conducive to the work God may want to accomplish in our lives.

No Quick Fixes

All advice should be carefully weighed. These are complex and difficult issues that have been addressed only briefly in this chapter. The very general thoughts here are my attempt to touch on the important ideas and lead you toward reading or counseling that can bring a more thorough analysis and understanding of your individual situation. Your husband's needs are complex and unique to him. It will take work and patience and love to understand his temptations and struggles and what shape your love might take to help him realize new strength and freedom.

Sometimes there is nothing you can do. Your help may be rejected. Or, as we have already seen, your support may only enable and contribute to the problem. Your husband may deny his struggle and refuse counsel. You will need wisdom to discern the level of harm in his behavior—to you, to him and to the rest of your family.

If the level of harm is not great, you may want to wait patiently and continue in prayer. God's timing is important in situations like these. Countless times I have seen men change because their wives were willing to stay with them through the dark period. Often it is some unexpected critical event that makes a man look at himself differently and finally be truly open to change. Sometimes by the natural process of aging a man will move into a new life stage that brings with it new awareness and a willingness to change. When Paul said that a wife should allow the unbelieving husband to stay with her, he must have had this hope in mind. Commitment to this kind of relationship takes patient love. I have seen God bless this kind of unique selflessness.

If your husband's behavior cannot be tolerated because it is harmful, then you have to act decisively to reduce the harm and create a new environment more conducive to change. A small group I was once a part of intervened in a difficult situation when an alcoholic husband we loved dearly would not seek the help he needed. Several from the group prayed with his wife, discussed the situation at great length and sought the counsel and help of a Christian psychiatrist. Our friend's health was an urgent, immediate concern, as was helping the couple in their marriage relationship. The group decided together out of love to intervene.

A place was arranged for the man at a local treatment center. Then members from the group just showed up at the house one night to take him to the center. He was surprised and angry at first. He would not agree that treatment was what he needed. The members from the group made it clear that they would not back down. Finally, he gave up his resisting and went with them to get the help he really needed. You can imagine how hard this was on these group members who loved the man and were his close friends. You can imagine, too, how hard this was for his wife to take this difficult stand to do what was necessary. And, of course, it was very difficult but courageous for our friend to admit his drinking problem and accept and cooperate with the program designed to treat his alcoholism.

Again, it is hard to know what kind of love will bring the help your spouse needs. Is it supportive, nurturing love that will coax him from the cocoon of his defenses? Or will your love need to be tough enough to help him take responsibility for his choices?

God, help us to accept peacefully the things we have no power to change, grant us the courage to change the things we can and bless us with your heavenly wisdom so we will know the difference.

APPENDIX
How to Stand Your Ground: Strategies for Beating Temptation

Now the serpent was more crafty
Than any of the wild animals
The Lord God had made.

GENESIS 3:1

I'll never forget the surprising experience I had one Sunday morning when a new student showed up in the university class. In the first minute I talked with her I experienced a powerful chemistry and attraction toward her. It bothered me immediately. I cut the conversation short and mixed with others in the group, but my mind kept drifting toward this young woman. I found myself thinking about her the rest of that Sunday and on into the next week.

One of the things that had helped me when I was a minister to university students was that I had matured to the place where I could relate freely and openly with college-aged women in an appropriate manner. I was old enough to be a good friend and even sometimes a kind of surrogate father for both the young men and young women in our university group.

Something was different with this woman. When she continued coming, I tried to sit at a distance from her, to avoid interacting in any way. At the same time I did all of the things I knew to take control and regain my equilibrium. But I still caught myself thinking about her too often.

There was another man working with me in the group whom I knew I could trust. I found some time with him and took the chance of sharing openly what I had been experiencing. To my astonishment, he told me that he too had been struggling with temptation related to this woman. And he felt other men were reacting in a similar way. We prayed together and promised to continue praying for each other. I also felt it was time to share this temptation with my wife. (I should have trusted her and included her sooner.) She supported me and prayed for me. Immediately following this time of confession and the forming of accountable relationships, I sensed an inner change and returned very quickly to my normal state of mind. I continued to be careful, but God had broken through.

Not until several weeks later did I come to understand more fully what had been taking place. The young woman gave her life to Christ. Most of us had not even known that she was not a Christian. There was a spiritual battle being waged for her soul. Satan was closing in for the kill and setting up a possible fall that could have damaged the lives and relationships of many in the group. Certainly any inappropriate behavior on my part or on the part of any other man toward this young woman would have impeded God's work.

We should have no illusions about it being a simple task to manage this difficult fight. It is impossible to coast. The devil is clever and subtle. It takes vigilance to stay out of danger. My experience with that young woman helped me to see again how vulnerable I am. We can be thankful to God when he shows us our weaknesses. It is only by the grace and power of God that we make headway day by day in this complex battle.

God has used the ideas I will mention in this chapter to make a difference for me at the critical moments when the pressure is on, or when I am suddenly surprised to find I have gotten myself into something and need help to get out. God has also used a number of these ideas to strengthen me to deal with the things that are tough daily battles. These are the attitudes that can help us create and sustain a lifestyle resistant to the powers that contend for a grip on our lives.

A Battle on Three Fronts

There are three dynamic elements which combine in varying degrees in situations of temptation we face: the self, the world and the devil. James explains the process through which temptation enters our lives when he writes: "But each one is tempted when, by his own evil desire, he is dragged away and enticed. Then, after desire has conceived, it gives birth to sin; and sin, when it is full-grown, gives birth to death" (Jas 1:14-15). James is saying that sin is conceived in our minds as a product of a connection between our lust and some worldly object. Lust having conceived brings forth sin. And sin when it is fully formed brings forth death. James gives us a picture of a kind of unholy trinity:

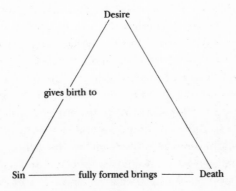

The Self

We engage temptation, as James describes it, when something in us responds to stimulation from outside. If there was nothing in us that could feel the draw toward worldly powers and pleasures, there would be no temptation. James calls this inner responsiveness "evil desire."

The reason we are drawn toward having the things of the world wrongly is that we are still dealing with that aspect of our old selves the Bible refers to as the flesh, or sinful nature (Rom 7:25; 8:5; Gal 5:19). In the verses listed here the Greek word *sarkos* meaning "flesh" connotes the sinful nature that resides in each of us—the flesh that is the seat of our willful desires. The apostle Paul recognized this power of the flesh operating in his life when he wrote, "For in my inner being I delight in God's law; but I see another law at work in the members of my body, waging war against the law of my mind and making me a prisoner of the law of sin at work within my members" (Rom 7:22-23).

All of us seek the fulfillment of our desires. The desires or yearnings we experience are not in themselves wrong. God has created the earth and all that is in it for our enjoyment and pleasure. What is wrong is that we often try to satisfy our cravings in ways that are inappropriate, unhealthy and contrary to God's will for our lives. This is what James calls "evil desire." It is the inner urging to fulfill our needs selfishly rather than God's way, wanting things and experiences according to our timing and to our chosen degree of satisfaction. We are reluctant to submit our needs and desires to the will and timing of God.

It is really a lack of trust in God that drives these evil desires. We believe we have to take what we need because we do not trust that God will really provide for our needs as he promises (Mt 6:25-34). But every time we take something to which we have no right, or take a good gift in the wrong way, we can expect a fall. And when we fall, we get hurt and we usually hurt others as well. All sin has negative consequences that reverberate through our life circle like ripples on the surface of a pool, touching our inner life of emotions, our outer life of relationships and, most significantly, diminishing the quality of our lives with God.

Someone has written, "Lust says I must have it now; but love says I can wait." It is our responsibility to manage and discipline the desires God has created in us. We do this because we love God. Learning to wait for God's healthy satisfaction of our basic needs is the key to contented living.

The World

The next element that plays a significant part in temptation is the world. The world is a smorgasbord of objects and experiences that engage our desires. It is when an inner desire we have attaches itself lustfully to an object or experience in the world that desire grows toward sin. James says we are "enticed" by something outside ourselves. The Greek word here is rooted in the language of fishermen. It means we are "lured, baited." When the bait is attractive to us, we may suddenly find ourselves seeking some selfish satisfaction.

The fault is not in the objects themselves. God's creation is not evil in itself. It is when we grasp something in the world with a self-seeking and self-indulgent spirit that sin occurs. The world is ours to enjoy as a gift from God. If we can manage our desires for the things in God's creation, not allowing ourselves to be controlled by the power of these pleasures, our interactions with the world can bring us true satisfaction along with spiritual and physical health and vitality. But if we are enslaved by our desires and we give our hearts to the things of the world without regard to God, we will suffer the consequences of sin in our lives.

The Devil

It is difficult for many today to believe that the devil and his subordinate devils really exist. The numerous verses in the Bible about the devil, Satan and evil spirits are often explained away today by both Christians and non-Christians as objects of projection. The psychology is that men and women will try to find something outside themselves to blame for their inner weaknesses and evil desires. And so they create evil beings to blame for their thoughts and actions. The biblical texts about the devil and demons are said to simply reflect the ignorance of the people in biblical times to the complexity and power of mental illness and the role of the subconscious mind.

One friend of mine believed wholeheartedly in the Bible and accepted the biblical narratives as true, but he interpreted all material related to the devil or to spirits as actually depicting the evil that lives within our psyche. For him Christ's temptation in the wilderness was really an interior monologue, rather than a description of Jesus interacting with an evil being. One day while studying together, we read the account in Matthew 8:28-34 where Jesus cast demons out of two possessed men. The narrative says that the demons pleaded with Jesus, asking him not to torture them, but to send them into a nearby herd of pigs. Jesus commands them to go. The demons enter the pigs, and the herd rushes down the embankment into the lake where the pigs drown in the water.

My friend read this passage through several times. Then instead of responding in his normal, predictable manner, he asked instead, "What went into the pigs?" For the first time he was faced with a biblical passage he could not explain according to his usual position. In this descriptive event, something passed from the men into the pigs and caused the animals to go crazy, rush into the lake and drown. My friend was forced by this account to consider the possibility that evil spiritual beings do exist and that they can act on us and in us to lead us away from God and promote the destruction of our lives.

The biblical doctrine of the devil would be hard for anyone

with more than a passing acquaintance of Scripture to ignore. A quick glance through any concordance shows the devil present from Genesis through Revelation. Scripture attests to the fact that he is in continual conflict with the people of God, tempting and accusing them, seeking to corrupt and destroy them and their witness to the truth of Jesus Christ (2 Cor 4:4; Rev 12:9-10; 1 Cor 5:5; Eph 2:2; 1 Thess 2:18; Mt 13:19). Perhaps it is enough to see where the apostle Paul believed the real battle was being waged. He wrote in Ephesians 6:10-12: "Finally, be strong in the Lord and in his mighty power. Put on the full armor of God so that you can take your stand against the devil's schemes. For our struggle is not against flesh and blood, but against the rulers, against the authorities, against the powers of this dark world and against the spiritual forces of evil in the heavenly realms."

If I were the devil, I would work very hard to convince the world that I did not exist. Then I would be able to accomplish my ends unhindered. If men and women did not believe in me, they would not resist me. It would be easier to keep them off-balance, frustrated and confused about why they are so driven by temptation and why they so often fail. This is what has happened in our day. Satan is thought of as a mythical character in a red suit with horns who lives in storybooks only and has about the same influence on the real world as other cartoon characters.

James says we are dragged away. This is forceful in the Greek. We see the bait. We are lured by it. Finally, we bite. Then we are swept away to our deaths. James would like us to see that there is an evil agent at work who can both create connections between our desires and the world and energize these connections with great intensity. Often, I am convinced, it takes nothing beyond our inner need or drive and the worldly object of our desire to create a situation ripe for sin. But it will help us all to remember that there is an evil being who is capable of bringing tremendous energy for destruction into the process of temptation.

Strategy One: Know Yourself

The first important way that we can begin to stand against the evil in our lives is to know ourselves and our weaknesses. Before Judie and I were Christians, we drank heavily. Judie was the first to bring up the idea that we might be problem drinkers. I denied it, fighting against the thought that I might not be able to control my drinking. It was not until I was able to admit that I had a problem that we both began gaining ground against it. Our struggles with drinking and our inability to manage it on our own was one of the things that first turned us toward Christ.

Are you able to admit the fact that something may have a hold on your life? What is it? Is it alcohol? Is it drugs? Is it the power of sex in pornography? Is it jealousy that drives you crazy? Is it your perfectionism? Is it another woman? Know your weaknesses before God or you will not know where to build your walls of defense. The most damaging weakness of all is the prideful refusal to admit weakness.

Pray that God will give you the courage to admit weakness. This is the first step toward change and often a very difficult one for men. Pray also that God will show you the weaknesses that could bring you or others harm. Sometimes, too, we try to deal with the shallower aspects of temptation and make little real progress because we do not understand the deeper needs we have that are not being met, but are the real roots of the recurring temptation. God can lead us into greater awareness and understanding of ourselves and our needs and show us why we have a hard time resisting certain things. If we listen carefully for his voice as we pray, read the Bible and interact with other Christians, he will speak. Keep a record of what he says.

A final important aspect of knowing ourselves is being aware

of our vulnerable times and regular patterns of certain temptations that gain ground in our lives. I know, for instance, that
I am more vulnerable to almost any temptation when I am
exhausted. Fatigue reduces my willpower and opens me up for
all kinds of things I would normally be able to resist. Knowing
this helps. If I need sleep, I try to get it. If instead I keep
pushing myself, I can expect to encounter temptation. Satan
will use our weaknesses against us.

A man I worked with in Wisconsin years ago struggled with
alcoholism. He always shopped at a grocery that had a liquor
store next door. He knew his vulnerability but placed himself
over and over again in a situation he could not resist. Don't
follow his example; instead try to understand yourself better in
order to learn how to avoid as much as possible putting yourself
into or letting yourself slip into no-win situations.

Strategy Two: Seek Renewal in the Spirit

Renewal comes to us as a gift from God. Any real and lasting
change cannot occur without new life through the Holy Spirit.
Renewal begins in repentance (2 Cor 7:10). God asks from us
an honest accounting of our sin and a willingness to respond
in obedience to his call. We will experience renewal as we
encounter God in genuine and deep repentance. We are never
closer to joy than we are when our hearts earnestly cry out for
his mercy and forgiveness. Grief over our sins is the beginning
of all new life and strength in the Lord.

Prior to starting this book, I went through what I recognize
now as about a two-year plateau with the Lord. My experience
was one of satisfaction with life in general and with my life in
God. Sure, I knew that there were things in my life with which
God must not be pleased, but life on the whole was going along
pretty well, and I developed some effective rationalizations and
defense mechanisms that allowed me to ignore the fact that
some things were on the slide. I had signed a contract to do

this book on temptation, but three months had gone by, and I had not written a word.

One morning I stayed home. Judie was working and the kids were in school. I walked around the house and out on the deck talking with God. I asked him why I was having so much trouble getting started on the book. I tried to tell God that I must be suffering from Satanic attack, battling a temptation not to write this book on temptation. But God was not listening to that line of reasoning. There might have been some truth in it, but there was something more important standing in the way. After I stopped telling God everything I was thinking, God started talking to me.

It was not long before I had a list of things on my notepad that God had brought to my mind as barriers to going ahead with the work on this book. Many of the things on the list were what I have thought of as "B" grade sins, the sins that are easier to live with because you know so many others who have similar problems, the sins that seem less destructive than a number of other sins you might have. But God was saying something different. He was showing me that my refusal to deal with these problem areas was hurting my relationship with him, standing in the way of my personal growth and blessing and making it impossible for me to write a book on the topic of resisting temptation. Writing on this topic while I was ignoring him in some important areas of my life was a hypocrisy God would not bless.

I repented. And God led me to make several covenants of obedience with him regarding my sin and my willingness to dig in and do something about it. My life was filled with new energy from God. However, almost immediately I began experiencing with greater intensity some of the temptations I had just given over to him. But I knew God would be faithful in strengthening me as I acted in obedience.

There was suddenly a new excitement in my life. On the one

hand it has been more difficult to face the things God has called me to deal with, but in another way, life has become easier. I am filled again with the joy of moving to higher levels of understanding and experience with the Lord. Perhaps this is what Jesus meant when he said: "Take my yoke upon you and learn from me, for I am gentle and humble in heart, and you will find rest for your souls. For my yoke is easy and my burden is light" (Mt 11:29-30). The yoke may be heavy; but Jesus can make it light.

I have learned again in my heart what I have known all along in my mind. Renewal begins in repentance and continues in obedience. And it is renewal that brings the joy of abundant living. The first thing that happened, of course, was that I was able to begin this book.

If you are serious about achieving progress with God against the temptations in your life, take your needs and weaknesses before God in prayer. Without repentance and obedience we remain mired in mediocrity, chained in the bondage of a visionless life. God cannot give us the blessings of faith until we take steps toward him. This is the only way to know God's peace and power at the deeper levels.

Strategy Three: Build a Strong Life Context

Acts 2:42-47 is a brief passage that describes the dynamic and growing early church. These new believers knew how to stay strong in Christ. They devoted themselves to the apostles' teaching, to fellowship with one another, sharing meals together and encouraging each other with the good news about what Jesus was doing to build his church. They met together to worship in the temple courts. They devoted themselves to prayer. They shared the Lord's supper. They served God in the church and in the world, having such a good influence upon their neighbors that the text says they "enjoyed the favor of all the people."

This is a good prescription for spiritual health and vitality. Today we devote ourselves to the apostles' teaching by hearing the Word of God taught and preached. "Consequently, faith comes from hearing the message, and the message is heard through the word of Christ" (Rom 10:17). Faith is confidence in God; we get that confidence by reading Scripture, by seeing how God has worked in the lives of other believers, and by experiencing the work of God in our own lives. Faith is taking control over fear and doubt by engaging our minds, thinking clearly about what we know is true about God. The Scripture says that "by faith Moses was able to resist the pleasures of Egypt" (Heb 11:24-26). Peter says that believers "through faith are shielded by God's power until the coming of the salvation that is ready to be revealed in the last time" (1 Pet 1:5).

Another good way to expose ourselves to Scripture is in small-group Bible studies. Being in relationships helps us to stay accountable to the truth we are learning from the Bible. We also want to be regularly involved in individual study of God's Word. Luke admired the Bereans who he said "were of more noble character than the Thessalonians, for they received the message with great eagerness and examined the Scriptures every day to see if what Paul said was true" (Acts 17:11).

The early church put a great premium on fellowship. The Greek word for fellowship, *koinonia,* is derived from *koinoneo,* which means "to share." New Testament believers shared their lives with one another, loving and caring for each other, encouraging and strengthening their fellow believers. This is also an important practice for us today. If we spend more time with the world than with the things of Christ, we will tend to pick up the values and patterns of worldly living. But spending time with other believers will strengthen us for kingdom living.

We have a men's retreat each year in our congregation where about two hundred men take a weekend together to learn and grow and build their faith. Each year while the retreat is happening, I cannot help but think of all the men who do not take advantage of this excellent weekend opportunity. Some men tell me they cannot work the weekend into their busy schedules, and I hear later that they went skiing or to a ball game. Be open to what God might want to do to strengthen you through good fellowship opportunities.

Some of the deepest and most important sharing we will do with others in the church is the sharing of confession of sin and developing relationships of accountability. James says, "Confess your sins to each other and pray for each other so that you may be healed" (Jas 5:16). There is probably nothing as damaging to our Christian lives as unconfessed sin. But it is often the only thing that can get us beyond something that holds us in bondage. My experience of trusting others with the struggles I have has been very good. Usually the confession to another opens up the possibility for the other person to share something as well. It is exciting to become prayer partners, upholding each other in the fight to break the bondage a sin holds on our lives.

The early Christians devoted themselves to prayer. Jesus modeled the importance of prayer in his own life. Mark 1:21-35 describes a day in the life of Jesus. After an incredible day of teaching and ministering healing to many, the passage ends with: "Very early in the morning, while it was still dark, Jesus got up, left the house and went off to a solitary place, where he prayed." Like any other relationship, our relationship with God will suffer if we do not spend time with him. If Jesus needed time with the Father, how much more should we seek this time with him? Each of us requires for our health a regular personal time of worship, of giving ourselves to God in confession and thanksgiving, of pouring out our needs and the needs of others to our Father and of listening to his guidance and help for our lives.

Having a place of service will also strengthen us. Having

work to do for God will keep us involved in the things of God and protect us from drifting. One friend of mine has gone through complex life changes, problems with business, and a host of other unsettling experiences. But he says one thing he will not give up is his commitment to serving God. His testimony is that God continues to keep him strong as he is engaged in the work of Christ. If you are not living out your commitment, think about your gifts and what you might be able to do to serve him. If you do have a place of service, resist the temptation to give this up when the going gets rough.

The last important piece in our foundation for strength in the Lord is learning to cooperate with the Holy Spirit's work in your life. We learn to "live by the Spirit" (Gal 5:16) as the Spirit builds discipline into our lives. Galatians 5:22 says, "The fruit of the Spirit is . . . self-control." The Spirit will help us live effectively. Make a thorough study of the power and blessings of the Holy Spirit. Paul says, "The mind of sinful man is death, but the mind controlled by the Spirit is life and peace" (Rom 8:6).

Strategy Four: Know Your Enemy

Our paradigm for the process of temptation is the serpent's work with Eve at the beginning. God had clearly commanded Adam and Eve not to eat or touch the fruit from the tree in the middle of the garden. Then the serpent enlists Eve in dialog about the command by saying, "Did God really say, 'You must not eat from any tree in the garden?' " (Gen 3:1). More significant here than the slant of the serpent's opening question is the fact that Eve enters into the conversation. Her right response would have been to say something like, "You have no authority to speak with me about the things that concern Adam, me and God." Instead, she stumbles, submitting her rightful authority to the serpent.

The serpent has put doubt about God in Eve's mind. Eve tells the serpent what God said—that they were not to eat the fruit from the tree in the middle of the Garden, or they would die. But the serpent reinterprets God's words for Eve. He tells her, "You will not surely die." And he adds, "For God knows that when you eat of it your eyes will be opened, and you will be like God, knowing good and evil" (vv. 4-5). In two brief lines he has called God a liar, pictured God as a kind of devil, jealous and protective of his position, and he has turned God's curse into a beckoning blessing in Eve's imagination. She is attracted to the look of the fruit and the idea that in eating it she will become like God. Eve eats. Then she becomes the devil's advocate. She offers the fruit to Adam. He eats. The Fall is complete.

With us, too, the first thing Satan will try to do is to engage us in dialog about sin and create doubt about what God may have really said or meant. His strategy is to give our minds ample opportunity to connect some craving with an attractive object in the world. If this connection and mental development did not occur, we would never sin.

It is quite normal for us to have the mental experience of a desire fixing itself to an object of satisfaction. We can control our thinking to some degree by keeping our minds engaged in thoughts about the good things of God. But we will often experience in our minds this sudden meeting between a craving and an attractive worldly object, which is not easily controlled.

The trick of Satan at this point is to build on that initial connection with dialog: "Did God really say that?" It is a subtle, seductive ploy. It opens the door to rationalization. We may suddenly find ourselves considering why a certain action would not be wrong in this particular case, even though it might be against God's will in general. It is hard to beat Satan in a debate. The best response is always to drive the dialog out of our minds and choose to talk with God instead. If we cannot make this mental break, lust will conceive and give birth to sin.

Another part of Satan's strategy with Eve was the promise of fulfillment—going against God's will would really be stepping into a new state of awareness, receiving the integration of her personality at a higher level. This is his essential strategy against us. We are told by the devil that if we have the thing we desire it will make us whole and bring the satisfaction and happiness that we feel we lack. How can we be so foolish as to believe that something good can come from something evil?

There are many seductive trails on the map of this temptation. First, there is an appeal to our flesh; the part of us that is still connected with the world is most vulnerable to the lie that the world will bring fulfillment. Our minds play with ideas like the following: Life is passing you by. You may not have this opportunity again. You deserve it. You've worked hard and have been good for quite a while. Reward yourself. You won't regret it. Others are doing it. They seem to get a lot out of it.

Next, our minds create a picture of what the experience will be like and how we will feel after having it. This undoubtedly happened to Eve. She must have imagined ahead of time what it would be like to be like God. God has gifted us with imagination and gives us vision to help us conceive of and accomplish new work in him. But Satan is able to twist this gift and use it for his ends. Our minds create a picture of the pleasure of sin. We think selectively about the pleasures of sinful experience. Our minds center on all the most enjoyable aspects and dwell on them. We ignore the ugly side of the sin and its damaging consequences.

I remember as a young boy ordering a pair of binoculars for three dollars through a magazine ad. The list of quality materials, exciting features and extraordinary optical specifications filled half a page. And there was a full refund if not satisfied. How could I lose? I waited three months for them to come in the mail. While I waited, the dozens of excellent features and how I would make use of each one ran through my mind.

When the binoculars finally arrived, they were a cheap plastic toy with glass lenses. I learned a good lesson about what you get for nothing. But the thing that has stuck with me the most was how my imagination ran wild while waiting for those glasses.

This experience reminds me of the power of our minds to predispose us to sin by fantasizing about what it will be like to finally have the object of our desires. In reality the actual sin experienced is never more than a pale shadow of what we held so long in our mind's eye, and the act is always followed by the negative consequences we chose not to consider.

Satan is able to twist our minds even more. As he leads us to dwell on the pleasurable aspects of some contemplated sin, he turns our minds at the same time to all the negative aspects of right action under God. Suddenly the sin seems so attractive; following God so dull. The very fact that the sinful thing is forbidden adds a sense of excitement to the thought of it. We begin to feel the exhilaration of self-assertion.

Satan is very skillful in this manipulation. Take, for instance, the temptation a man might experience for an attractive woman at work. While he thinks about the high degree of pleasure he would receive from a physical relationship with her, he is thinking at the same time about the unfulfilling sexual experience he had with his wife the night before. She was exhausted. He laid a guilt trip on her about it, so she gave in to him half-heartedly. But this other woman seems so energetic. She would never be tired at night. Beware. Men who fall for this kind of mental seduction usually wind up trading a good and growing relationship for a hornet's nest of new problems. The aim here is to be aware that both God and Satan can work through the power of mind. Guard your mind.

We know that sin is often pleasurable. If there was no pleasure in it, it would not be attractive to us. Another trick of Satan is to bring the greatest experience of pleasure into the first occasion of a particular sensual sin. But Satan has given all he has in the initial experience. What follows always falls far short, yet we pursue the sin repeatedly, hoping to duplicate the experience at the same or at an increased level of intensity. If I snort cocaine for a while and the pleasure diminishes, I try smoking crack. A friend of mine who used to dabble in psychedelic drugs, and then later became addicted to heroin, told me his first experience with the harder drug gave him the rush he could no longer get from the lesser drugs. But he then described his addiction over the long haul as "one big high, and the rest was killing pain." Bondage to Satan always produces in us a greater and greater appetite for a steadily decreasing pleasure. It is the same story in so many areas of our lives: we must have the more prestigious car, the bigger house, the more complex and powerful deal with its big-money pay-off.

God never manipulates. He will not use experiences of pleasure or power to seduce us into acting against our will. Our lives in him remind me of what the guests said about the wedding host when Jesus turned his water into wine. They remarked that the host saved his best wine for last.

God's pleasures do not have negative side effects. The longer we follow God, the more our sense of pleasure in him grows. The pleasures of God are both of the Spirit and of the things in creation. When God says no to something, it is not to diminish our pleasure, but to enhance it. If we hold this foremost in our thinking, it is unlikely that we will become fools. He wants us to know how good and satisfying life can be when it is received in his will and enjoyed according to his timing.

Strategy Five: Motivate Yourself for Right Living

I have found that a few basic thoughts help motivate me in the fight. High on my list is the idea that this world is not my home. The apostle Peter encourages us in this kind of thinking when he writes, "live your lives as strangers here in reverent fear" (1

Pet 1:17). If we really believed in eternal life, would we put so much of our energy into obtaining everything that the world has to offer? Could it be that we really believe deep down that this life is all there is and we better get all of it we can while the getting's good?

When my daughter Jana was six, she asked me one day if I didn't think it was wonderful that we would all die soon and go to heaven. I remember distinctly realizing that I did not feel as excited about it as she apparently did. Then she said in an encouraging tone, "Well, if we keep busy, it'll go fast." The beautiful thing about this is that this is exactly the way we should feel. If we internalize this truth, it will change how we live our lives. We will not spend so much time thinking about what we have to have or experience in this world before we move on. Our focus instead can be on the Lord and his work. We will be able to put off immediate gratification knowing the blessings that will soon be ours in glory.

Another thought that motivates me to continue to grow in Christ is the excitement of thinking of the new ways God can use me as I choose obedience and continue to grow in maturity and strength. We cannot see now what God has in store for our future lives. But if we stay at the same level with God, we can count on the fact that the quality and excitement of our Christian life will stay at the same level as well. If we move ahead in faith and obedience, God will go before us and open doors we never dreamed we could walk through. Let God have your life more completely, and you will see that he is able to use you increasingly in his work.

A third thing that I often think of when faced with a decision is how much might ride on it, even if it appears to be a small obedience. The temptation might be to ignore the person sitting next to you on the bus, even though she appears to be distressed. Think of the fact that choosing to enter into her life may bring healing and create an open door through which God can work. And if she becomes a Christian, think of the numerous others she might touch with the love of Christ. Think then of all those people reaching out to their families and friends. We often do not consider how even a small obedience—a kind word, returning a wallet to its rightful owner, refusing to blur the moral distinctions on a business deal—might over time and under the influence of the Spirit vastly affect the future work of God.

Good theology can also be a motivating factor. Grasping the practical application of the greatest commandment " 'Love the Lord your God with all your heart and with all your soul and with all your strength and with all your mind'; and 'Love your neighbor as yourself,' " can make all the difference for us if we keep it in mind. I simply cannot do the things that will hurt God if I really love him. And if I really love my neighbor, there is a host of things I can never do. I cannot covet his wife, not if I really love him and really love her. I cannot steal from my neighbor, or trick him or use another to get my way—not if I really love him.

Living with a vision is another motivating factor. Without a vision for our lives it is too easy for us to let the world squeeze us into its mold (Rom 12:2). We tell ourselves that everybody is doing it. This kind of thinking brings everyone down to the lowest common denominator. But the world needs strong men and women in Christ who will stand up for God, looking to him for a vision for living rather than giving in to the weaker lifestyles of those who court the world. Karl Barth said, "We must challenge the right of this passing age to set the agenda for our lives." We can let God guide us and give us the strength to be extraordinary in him, rather than ordinary. If we are looking to the world for our standards of behavior, we will always give in too soon, and we will always be smaller than we need to be.

Finally, there is a place for righteous anger. We can be angry about sin and the destruction it causes in the lives of those we love. Personalize your enemy—Satan. I find this to be a motivating factor. I can get up for a fight against this kind of evil.

Strategy Six: Beware of Strengths

Somerset Maugham has written a fascinating short story entitled "Rain." In it a ship is forced by continual driving rain to remain docked in a small native village for about two weeks. The passengers take lodging at a boarding house. One of the men, Pastor Davidson, a missionary, takes it upon himself to convert the local prostitute who has a room at the house. At the end of the story there is a shocking twist. When the boat is finally ready to leave, Pastor Davidson cannot be found. Even his wife has no idea where he might be. Then they hear the report that a local native has found a body on the beach. It was Davidson. He had cut his own throat with a razor. It is clear what has happened. The prostitute converted the minister.

One mistake we can easily make is to consider ourselves strong in an area when in reality we may simply have not been tested. I thank God daily for the numerous ways he protects me from experiencing temptation in situations that might be too tough for me to handle. Who among us would not find it difficult to resist wrong if the situation appealed to a deep need and came upon us at a vulnerable moment?

Even when we have stood the test in a specific area, we cannot be complacent. I love to fish for trout in the Colorado Rockies. When fishing with flies on a lake, there is often a powerful strike followed by a brief flurry of fight. Then the fish appears to give up as you drag it slowly toward you through the water. Sometimes it even swims toward you on shore or toward the boat. But I've learned not to let my guard down. Just before the fish is netted it will usually put up the strongest fight of all. I have come up empty again and again. Our temptations are like this. We will have a tremendous fight as we begin to tackle them. Then we gain ground and the fight slacks off. But if we think the fight is over, we can be in deep trouble. We can count on an even greater battle with the thing just before it is fully netted.

Colorado rock climbers have a saying they live by, "The summit is closest to the abyss." It is so easy as you near the summit to let up a bit and have a brief lapse of concentration. At that point the little error is often made, and that one small mistake can be fatal.

Another thing to remember is that our strengths all have a dark side. Strong leaders will be prone to grasp for power. Financial geniuses have to watch the way they manipulate money, especially in the church and for the Lord. Great preachers can motivate people for selfish rather than godly ends. And on the simplest level we often see good organizers trying to run everybody else's life, or good and gentle listeners who cannot get up the courage to confront others. What are your strengths and gifts? Think about their dark sides. What could you be tempted to do because of your gifts that would be contrary to God's will? Pray about these things regularly, and ask God to protect you.

Strategy Seven: Shift Energy Away from Temptations

Weakness lives in our overconcern with self. We become preoccupied with our pain, life's inconveniences and what we should have coming to us. This self-absorption creates in us an openness to self-indulgent sin. If we shift our energies toward God's work, helping others and thinking about them, many common temptations will have no foothold in our lives. Paul writes, "Whatever you do, work at it with all your heart, as working for the Lord, not for men" (Col 3:23). Many of our sins come from our conscious or unconscious need to reward ourselves. We are so manipulated by the world that we find ourselves living for the weekends. But Paul is saying that if we work for the Lord, it should carry its own reward.

Every day that we can do something for God and for others is a day in which we should find great enjoyment. The old saying "Idle hands are the devil's workshop" is really very true. Much of our problem with temptation and sin in this country is a function of the luxury of free time. Paul says to all of us, "clothe yourselves with the Lord Jesus Christ, and do not think about how to gratify the desires of the sinful nature" (Rom 13:14). This comes at the end of a passage in which Paul stresses the importance of redeeming the time we have been given by God. If we fill our lives more with the things of God, we will have less time to think about, plan for and gratify the desires of our flesh.

Strategy Eight: Don't Feed Your Cravings

If we feed a sin, the need for satisfaction and the control of the sin over us both grow. One of the areas in which I have noticed this in my life is with food. I am always more susceptible to overeating when I am in a period of overeating. And the more I eat, the less satisfied I seem to be. The way I control my eating is to regularly eat less and to say no before I have stuffed myself. Then I am less driven in my appetite for food. Our physical desires and our mental preoccupations both grow as we feed them. They will often diminish as we bring them under control. Single men have reported to me that making a decision not to mentally or physically feed their sexual drive has freed them from an obsession with sex. I believe them. It is possible in the Lord to be delivered from any obsession we may have.

Strategy Nine: Develop Good Habits

Habits are our predispositions to act predictably each time a certain set of circumstances arises. We all have good and bad habits. The good habits are the disciplines we have built into our lives through repeatedly acting in healthy and appropriate ways. As we take one area under control, the discipline we have gained through repeated action will begin to overflow into other areas. Our bad habits are usually formed through neglect. In this case, the lack of discipline encourages weakness. When we give up the fight in some area, we will soon see the weakness creeping into other areas as well. One great proverb reads, "A weak person is like a city broken into and left without walls" (Prov 25:28). As the blocks crumble in one area of the wall, it is usually not long before another area begins to give in as well. Soon we find that things which used to bother us no longer make us feel uncomfortable. Then we are in real danger.

We need to learn to say no. Each time we commit ourselves in an area, trusting the Lord to help us stand, and each time we make a choice consistent with our commitment, we build another block of strength into our walls of defense. With a good habit in place we no longer have to struggle to decide what to do each time we are confronted with a choice. Good habits make automatic our healthy responses for God.

Strategy Ten: Be Teachable

There is nothing worse than having to go through the same pain or struggle repeatedly because we have not learned how to incorporate new insight into our lives. There will always be struggle. There is no growth without it. "No discipline seems pleasant at the time, but painful," says the writer of Hebrews. "Later on, however, it produces a harvest of righteousness and peace for those who have been trained by it" (Heb 12:11). The Lord will discipline those he loves (Heb 12:6; Rev 3:19). Will we accept it?

It is easy to be blind to our need for growth. Jesus brought this problem into focus when he said, "Why do you look at the speck of sawdust in your brother's eye and pay no attention to the plank in your own eye?" (Mt 7:3). We can live our whole lives focused more on what others should be learning and doing than on the areas where we desperately need to experience life-change in the Lord.

Another of my favorite short stories is "A Good Man Is Hard to Find" by Flannery O'Connor. In it an elderly grandmother sees everything that everyone around her needs to do to improve, while seeing herself in the very best light. On a family vacation the grandmother suggests taking a back road. On that road they have an accident and are found by a group of escaped convicts who ruthlessly murder every member of the family. It is not until the moment of her death that the old woman has her first real spiritual insight—that she is really no better than the convicts who are murdering her family, that everyone is filled with sin, including herself, that a good man *is* hard to find. She reaches out to touch the shoulder of the convict who is about to kill her. He responds by shooting her three times in the chest. There is a great irony in the convict's closing comment to his friends: "She would of been a good woman if it had been somebody there to shoot her every minute of her life."

What does it take to get your attention? Having teachable spirits means that we will listen carefully to God as he speaks through Scripture and through those around us who know us well. Growing to maturity in Christ requires this kind of openness. If we resist, we can be sure that God will get our attention sooner or later. It is best to train ourselves to be receptive to God's work in us all along. And when we learn something we should really learn it, accept it, internalize it, decide to act upon it and remember it. It is a waste of time and pain to have to learn the same lesson over and over again.

Strategy Eleven: Run from Temptation
In the well-known story in Genesis 31 Joseph was entrusted by Potiphar with management of the household. All went well, except that Potiphar's wife wanted Joseph to sleep with her. He

refused. On one occasion he was in the house working. None of the other servants was present. Potiphar's wife grabbed Joseph by the cloak saying, "Come to bed with me!" Joseph leaves his cloak in her hand as he rushes out of the house.

Sometimes a sinful thought will captivate us. The best response is to close the mind to the thought, to run from it. Sometimes we will need to run, like Joseph did, from an actual opportunity for sin. We should not give in to a sin just because we might be embarrassed to run from it. Keep focused on the behavior, not on pleasing your peers. This takes courage.

My good friend Bill was recently offered a promotion. As he and the president of the company talked, the president described for him a nightclub setting where there might be a lingerie show (slightly covered nudity) or topless entertainment. The president said: "Now this wouldn't bother you, would it? We find that this kind of entertainment enhances our business." My friend simply replied that he did not believe such an atmosphere was really conducive to building the kind of clientele the company needed and that he would not want to take clients to that kind of place to do business. Bill did not get the job. He wanted the promotion and the new challenge very much. But he would not compromise his integrity to get it. He ran from the sin.

Strategy Twelve: Be Courageous

Jesus himself maligns the cowardly (Rev 21:8). We should develop the habit of putting up a good fight against sin and Satan.

One thing that takes courage is choosing to act against something that is currently controlling us. As I mentioned in an earlier chapter, I subscribed to *Playboy* for a number of years before I became a Christian. A few days after committing my life to Christ, I carried several years' worth of magazines to the alley and dumped them in the trash. It was not easy. I had favorite issues. But it felt so good to choose to destroy that which exerted its twisted control over my life.

I have had to take action against other things in a similar way since becoming a Christian. I highly recommend it. Are you in bondage, under the control of something outside yourself? Get tough. Exert more power over the temptation than it is exerting over you. Burn the books or magazines. Erase the videotapes. Dump the liquor or flush the drugs. Do not contact that woman again. Oh, I know that the external reality is only one part of the problem. But when your external action accompanies authentic inner repentance and a deep desire to be made new in an area of struggle, taking a bold step can go a long way toward breaking through to freedom.

It takes a great deal of courage to be willing to make each battle against temptation a fight to the finish. I love football. It absolutely amazes me how the players will suck it up and keep on playing even after a serious injury. You hear stories all the time of an offensive lineman playing with a broken leg or about a linebacker breaking his ribs in the first quarter and going back into the game with a flak jacket on in the second half. In reality it is probably more foolish than sensible for a player to feel that he has to give that much for a game. But at the same time I have often said to myself that this is the way I want to live the Christian life. I want to learn to play hurt, to endure pain to reach the goal, to get up again and again after Satan thinks he has me pinned to the turf.

As Christian men, we should be heroes of hardship. Sure we will lose some of the battles, but we will come back fighting, earning the reputation of being men who are willing to play even when hurt. Solomon wrote, "The righteous man falls seven times, and rises again" (Prov 24:16). It would do us all good to read and reread the stories of the faithful of Hebrews 11. Through faith "weakness was turned to strength" in these men and women of God (v. 34). Remembering pain may weaken us. But hope is stronger than memory. And God has given us every reason to believe that it is worth running this difficult race.

Paul writes: "No temptation has seized you except what is common to man. And God is faithful; he will not let you be tempted beyond what you can bear. But when you are tempted, he will also provide a way out so that you can stand up under it" (1 Cor 10:13). Each time we take the fight to the limit, God builds our strength and courage a quantum leap.

There is a catch to the promise above. The verse says God will not let us be tempted beyond our capacity to resist. But as we grow in Christ, our capacity to withstand grows as well. We can expect to face greater temptations as we progress in God. It is the only way we can keep growing and building our strength to full maturity.

It takes tremendous courage to live the Christian life.

Is There Anything Good in Temptation?

God does not tempt us. But through encounters with temptation we do gain strength in Christ. This is the first good thing that results from our struggle with temptation. The experience of real character development gives us hope. We know God is in our lives when we can measure the progress of real life-change over time. Paul says this in Romans 5:3-4, "We also rejoice in our sufferings, because we know that suffering produces perseverance; perseverance, character; and character, hope." James adds a similar wisdom, when he writes: "Consider it pure joy, my brothers, whenever you face trials of many kinds, because you know that the testing of your faith develops perseverance. Perseverance must finish its work so that you may be mature and complete, not lacking anything" (Jas 1:2-4). It is a great joy to experience new life as we grow toward maturity in Christ.

There is a second good thing that results from our struggle with temptation. In *Temptation,* Charles Durham argues that our personal temptation is a divine demonstration to the powers of the universe that teaches God's character and work. The story of Job pictures this incredible reality. At the beginning of the book of Job Satan brings a challenge to God. God allows him to put Job to the test. Job is tempted to doubt God, to turn away from God, and even to take his own life. But he stands fast. The good in the Job story is not just in his own strength in the Lord. His battle against temptation and his courage to stand in the strength of God against all odds proved the power of faith to devils and angels alike. It was a decisive victory for God.

Another passage which furthers this demonstration theme has Jesus telling Simon Peter: "Satan has asked to sift you as wheat. But I have prayed for you, Simon, that your faith may not fail. And when you have turned back, strengthen your brothers" (Lk 22:31-32). Here again there is a dialog between heaven and hell and an important test of personal faith observed. God's chosen are living out day by day a battle that proves to heavenly and earthly spiritual beings who God is and what he has accomplished in Christ.

Temptation is a personal struggle that both refines our character and proves to the powers of heaven and earth that we are truly new creatures in Christ. As important as our growth toward holiness is, there is even more at stake. In Ephesians 3:10-11 Paul encapsulates for us the significance of the faithful activity of God's church: "His intent was that now, through the church, the manifold wisdom of God should be made known to the rulers and authorities in the heavenly realms, according to his eternal purpose which he accomplished in Christ Jesus our Lord."

Our successful struggle against temptation accomplishes far more than we can imagine. Let this truth unite us, strengthening us to fight the good fight and demonstrate to the watching powers that the resurrection energy God exerted in Jesus when he raised him from the dead now empowers faithful men to win strength out of weakness.

Questions for Groups and Individuals

1. Which of the three elements—the self, the world, the devil (p. 227)—do you recognize as being most involved in your experiences of temptation? least involved?

2. Knowing yourself is an important factor in battling temptation. Are there certain circumstances that bring out your particular weaknesses and make you especially vulnerable to temptation? What are they?

3. Why do you think it is important for Christians to be honest with each other about their struggles with temptation?

4. On a scale of one to ten (one being closed, ten being open), how good do you think you are at being honest about your struggles with at least one other Christian? If possible, relate an experience where openly confiding in a fellow believer helped you to triumph over temptation.

5. James says that "after desire has conceived, it gives birth to sin." What are some of the ways we respond to initial desires that are not productive and can lead us into sin?

What are some responses to desires that can help us to manage the desires more effectively?

6. This chapter presents a wide variety of motivating ideas to help us choose right living. Which of the ideas in the chapter do you think will be most helpful to you?

7. The author points out that our strengths and gifts have dark sides and may themselves contribute to sin in our lives. (p. 246) Give an example of a strength you have that could possibly lead you into sinful choices.

Notes

Preface
[1]Joseph R. McAuliffe, "Why Men Fail," *Chalcedon Report*, June 1988, p. 12.

Chapter One: Set Free
[1]Used by permission of James Croegaert, 827 Monroe, Evanston, Ill. 60202. © 1982, all rights reserved.
[2]C. S. Lewis, *The Voyage of the Dawn Treader* (New York: Collier Books, 1970), p. 93.
[3]Used by permission of Bob Sheffield, The Navigators, Colorado Springs, Colo.
[4]C. S. Lewis, *Letters of C. S. Lewis* (New York: Harcourt Brace Jovanovich, 1975), p. 199.

Chapter Two: The Temptation to Be Macho
[1]James Wagenvoord, ed., *Men: A Book for Women* (New York: Avon Books, 1978), p. 165.
[2]George Gilder, *Men and Marriage* (Gretna: Pelican Publishing Company, 1987), chap. 1.
[3]Margaret Mead, *Male and Female: A Study of the Sexes in a Changing World* (New York: Dell, 1968), p. 168.
[4]George Gilder, *Men and Marriage*, p. 180.
[5]Leonard Woolf, *The Journey Not the Arrival Matters* (New York: Harcourt, Brace & World, Inc., 1969), p. 158.
[6]James B. Nelson, *The Intimate Connection* (Philadelphia: Westminster Press, 1988), pp. 98-99.

James Nelson raises an important issue which is problematic for the androgyny position. He shows that androgyny is the solution posed by many to reduce the tension men and women feel at having to live out traditional stereotypes of male and female roles that seem unnatural for them. But the androgyny solution has some problems. Those who take the androgyny position claim that both feminine and masculine characteristics are a part of every individual and both should be developed and expressed. Nelson writes:

> But this can be oppressive in its own way. Now each person has two sets of gender traits to learn and incorporate instead of one. Now everyone is expected to acquire thoroughly both "instrumental/agentic" ("masculine") and "expressive/nurturant" ("feminine") characteristics in equal amounts, a standard that would seem to double the pressure that people traditionally have felt.

Even more basically, another problem is that androgyny is based on the assumption that there are, indeed, two distinct and primordial sets of personality characteristics—one "masculine," the other "feminine." Even if we assume that each sex is capable of developing both sets of traits, the definition itself perpetuates the very problem it had hoped to overcome. It still locates one constellation of qualities essentially and dominantly in men and the other constellation essentially and dominantly in women.

The problem is that androgyny assumes as its basis the very idea it is trying to overcome, that there are primary and distinctive masculine and feminine characteristics. The program of androgyny would not exist if this weren't true about men and women.

Nelson's book is a helpful study that takes us farther in understanding masculinity. His controlling idea is that a healthy understanding of what it means to be a man can be gained by trying to see more clearly the broad implications that grow out of the male physiology. He argues that a truly healthy masculinity is not obtained by trying to add feminine qualities to our masculinity. This would be like learning a second language. We can do it, but the second language is never really ours. Instead, Nelson sees that a full range of personality possibilities including everything from tough assertiveness to gentle vulnerability is powerfully symbolized and grounded in our male bodies through our rhythmic experience of the hardness of phallus and the softness of penis. This takes some development in the book, but the work is well thought out and helpful. Primary to the position is the importance of seeing that a broad range of personality characteristics is really rooted in our masculinity. The gentler qualities are not feminine qualities unnatural to us and outside of our realm of experience that in some way have to be tacked on.

The book is worth studying because it takes a step forward in understanding the full dimension of masculinity that is grounded in our male physiology. The reader will have to read with care when Nelson addresses the homosexual issues. Here he misses by sidestepping relevant Scripture and refusing to deal honestly with the obvious intent of God that marriage be the bond between a man and a woman and that sexuality has to account for the importance of procreation in God's design or it is irresponsible sex.
[7]Gilder, *Men and Marriage.*

Gilder is worth reading, both to understand the implications of androgyny for our society, and for his research into the biological and chemical reasons behind why men are men and women are women. His concern is that the sexual revolution and breakdown of tradition sex roles has led to a deterioration of the family structure on which all productive societies are built. His research into the biological and chemical realities of male and female is to support his thesis that some traditional views about the sexes are more than simply social conventions. These are issues Gilder believes are critical to the survival of a healthy social order.

[8]Harold M. Voth, "Women's Liberation, Cause and Consequence of Social Sickness," *New Oxford Review,* December 1980, pp. 8-10.

[9]James B. Nelson, *The Intimate Connection,* p. 100.

Chapter Three: The Temptation of Sexual Lust

[1]Anonymous, "The War Within: An Anatomy of Lust," *Leadership* 3 (Fall 1982):30ff.

[2]Anonymous, "The War Within Continues," *Leadership* 9 (Winter 1988):24ff.

[3]J. R. Braun, *The Meaning of Sexual Pleasure* (St. Paul: Genesis 2, 1976), p. 34.

[4]Braun, *The Meaning,* p. 163.

[5]Dr. Jerry R. Kirk, *The Mind Polluters,* available with other extensive information on pornography from The National Coalition Against Pornography, Inc.; 800 Compton Rd.; Suite 9248; Cincinnati, Ohio 45231.

[6]For a more complete and informative biblical and historical discussion of homosexual behavior, see John Jefferson Davis, *Evangelical Ethics* (Phillipsburg, N.J.: Presbyterian and Reformed Publishing Company, 1985), pp. 106-128.

[7]Kim McDonald, "Sex Under Glass," *Psychology Today,* March 1988, p. 59.

[8]David Ratcliff, "Responsible Sex and the Christian Single," *United Presbyterian Church Single Adult Publication,* Winter 1988, p. 4.

[9]Dr. Joyce Brothers, "The Myth of the Trial Marriage," *New Woman,* March 1985, pp. 54-57.

Chapter Four: The Temptation to Have an Affair

[1]Laurel Richardson, "Another World," *Psychology Today,* February 1986, p. 22.

[2]"How Common Is Pastoral Indiscretion?" *Leadership* 10 (Winter 1988):12-13.

[3]Dr. James C. Dobson, *Straight Talk to Men and Their Wives* (Waco, Tex.: Word, 1980), p. 44.

[4]I am deeply indebted for this material to my friend and colleague in ministry, Dr. Jay Lindsay, a Christian psychologist in Boulder, Colorado, whose creative work and seminar entitled "People Helping and the Extramarital Affair" has helped me greatly to have a practical grasp of how affairs happen in the lives of Christians. The "Twelve Step Affair Process" is based on Dr. Lindsay's work and used here with his permission.

[5]*Journal of Family Issues* 6 (September 1985):277. Close to seventy per cent of second marriages end in divorce. Thirty-five per cent of first marriages end in divorce. The well-known figure of fifty per cent of all marriages ending in divorce is derived from a combination of the statistics from these two groups.

[6]H. Norman Wright, *Understanding the Man in Your Life* (Waco, Tex.: Word, 1987), pp. 142-145.

Chapter Five: The Temptation to Wield Power

[1]John Stott, as quoted from *Ephesians: Mastering the Basics,* Lyman Coleman and Richard Peace (Littleton: Serendipity, 1986), p. 54.

Chapter Six: The Temptation to Love Money

[1]Mlle. Moussat, Bulletin Jeune Femme, July 1952, found in Jacques Ellul, *Money and Power* (Downers Grove: InterVarsity Press, 1984), p. 31.

[2]W. A. Smart, "Christianity and Wealth," *Christianity and Wealth* (Cincinnati: Methodist Church Literature, May 1954), p. 7.

[3]A good book on this issue is *Wealth and Poverty: Four Christian Views of Economics,* ed. Robert G. Clouse (Downers Grove: InterVarsity Press, 1984).

[4]Pilgrim, *Good News to the Poor,* p. 174, quoted from Robert G. Clouse, *Wealth and Poverty* (InterVarsity Press: Downers Grove, 1984), p. 223. The three priorities mentioned in this last section come from a postscript of the Robert Clouse book.

Chapter Seven: The Temptation to Be Perfect

[1]J. I. Packer, consulting ed., *The New Bible Dictionary* (Grand Rapids: Eerdmans, 1974), p. 967.

[2]Dr. David Stoop, *Living with a Perfectionist* (Kansas City: Thomas Nelson, 1987), pp. 31-76.

[3]David D. Burns, "The Perfectionist's Script for Self-Defeat," *Psychology Today,* November 1980, pp. 34-41.

[4]Ibid., p. 34.

[5]Ibid.

[6]Ibid.

[7]Ibid., p. 37.

[8]Thomas J. Peters and Robert H. Waterman, Jr., *In Search of Excellence* (New York: Harper and Row, 1982), p. 223.

[9]Dietrich Bonhoeffer, *Life Together* (New York: Harper and Row, 1954), p. 27.

[10]Ibid.

Chapter Eight: Deliverance

[1]C. S. Lewis, *The Weight of Glory* (New York: Macmillan, 1980), pp. 3-4.

[2]Taken from Alcoholics Anonymous, published by A. A. World Services, New York, N.Y., pp. 59-60.

Chapter Nine: How Can I Help My Man? A Chapter for Women

[1]Dr. James Dobson, *Love Must Be Tough* (Waco: Word, 1983), p. 45.